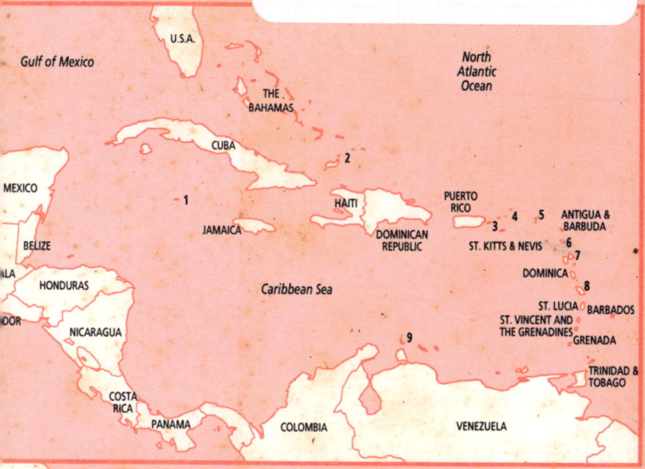

1 Cayman Islands
2 Turks & Caicos
3 US Virgin Islands
4 UK Virgin Islands
5 Anguilla
6 Montserrat
7 Guadeloupe
8 Martinique
9 Netherlands Antilles

POCKET LATIN AMERICA AND THE CARIBBEAN

OTHER TITLES FROM
THE ECONOMIST BOOKS

The Economist on America: 1843–1993
The Economist Numbers Guide
The Economist Style Guide

Pocket Finance
Pocket Manager
Pocket Marketing
Pocket MBA
Pocket Negotiator
Pocket Strategy

The Economist Pocket Asia
The Economist Pocket Europe
The Economist Pocket USA
The Economist Pocket World in Figures

The Economist

POCKET

LATIN AMERICA AND THE CARIBBEAN

Roland Dallas

THE ECONOMIST IN ASSOCIATION WITH
HAMISH HAMILTON LTD

Published by the Penguin Group
Penguin Books Ltd, 27 Wrights Lane, London W8 5TZ, England
Penguin Books USA Inc., 375 Hudson Street, New York,
New York 10014, USA
Penguin Books Australia Ltd, Ringwood, Victoria, Australia
Penguin Books Canada Ltd, 10 Alcorn Avenue, Toronto,
Ontario, Canada M4V 3B2
Penguin Books (NZ) Ltd, 182–190 Wairau Road, Auckland 10,
New Zealand

Penguin Books Ltd, Registered Offices: Harmondsworth,
Middlesex, England

First published by Hamish Hamilton Ltd in association
with The Economist 1994

1 3 5 7 9 10 8 6 4 2

Additional research: Peter Holden

Printed in Great Britain by William Clowes Limited,
Beccles and London

A CIP catalogue record for this book is available
from the British Library

ISBN 0-241-00262-1

Contents

7 **Introduction**

17 **Part I Country Rankings**

18 **Size and society**
Area
Population
Population growth
Population density
Youngest populations
Human development index

20 **Living standards**
Life expectancy: men
Life expectancy: women
Infant mortality
Doctors and patients
Literacy
People per telephone
People per TV

22 **The economy**
GDP
GDP per head
Purchasing power
GDP change
Agriculture's contribution to GDP
Inflation
Debt
Debt as % of GDP
Debt service

25 **Part II Central America Country Profiles**

26 Belize
30 Costa Rica
34 El Salvador
38 Guatemala
42 Honduras
46 Mexico
52 Nicaragua
56 Panama

61 **Part III Caribbean Country Profiles**

62 Anguilla
64 Antigua
66 The Bahamas

68 Barbados
70 Bermuda
72 Cayman Islands
74 Cuba
80 Dominica
82 Dominican Republic
86 Grenada
88 Guadeloupe
90 Haiti
94 Jamaica
98 Martinique
100 Montserrat
102 Netherlands Antilles and Aruba
104 Puerto Rico
108 St Kitts and Nevis
110 St Lucia
112 St Vincent and the Grenadines
114 Trinidad & Tobago
118 Turks and Caicos Islands
120 Virgin Islands (UK)
122 Virgin Islands (US)

125 **Part IV South America Country Profiles**

126 Argentina
134 Bolivia
140 Brazil
148 Chile
154 Colombia
160 Ecuador
164 French Guiana
166 Guyana
170 Paraguay
174 Peru
180 Suriname
184 Uruguay
188 Venezuela

194 **Glossary**
198 **Notes on data**
200 **Sources**

INTRODUCTION

For most of its history, Latin America has been on the margin of world affairs. More often than not, it has been ignored or forgotten except at times when it suffers from a financial, political or social crisis. Whenever the world's major powers have taken important decisions, Latin America's voice has gone unheard. This is still more or less the case today. But Latin America is changing. It has adopted political and economic policies which, if implemented thoroughly, will set the countries of the region on the road to stable economic growth leading to political stability and a narrowing of the gap between rich and poor. If this can be achieved, and it is now possible though by no means certain, Latin American leaders will have won the right to demand a hearing from the rest of the world.

A unique mixture

For most of its history, the western hemisphere south of the Rio Grande has lived under authoritarian rule. The Aztecs in Mexico and the Incas in Peru lived under strict codes. Montezuma in Mexico and Atahualpa in Peru were no believers in democracy. Nor were their successors, Hernan Cortes and Francisco Pizarro, both *conquistadores* whose purpose was to achieve glory, grab land for themselves and establish the secular authority of the king of Spain and the spiritual dominion of the Roman Catholic Church. They were successful. In many parts of the region, Spanish and Portuguese colonists became great landowners; the local inhabitants were called Indians but in fact people of many races, languages and cultures worked for them. Many were little more than slaves. In other parts of the region, such as Argentina, the indigenous population was killed off. Those who survived often did so as a beaten people bereft of national identity. Millions still speak ethnic languages throughout the region.

A shining example

The slave trade brought Africans to the islands of the Caribbean, the Caribbean coast of Central America, Colombia, Venezuela and Brazil, where they worked on sugar plantations. First of the predominantly black countries to attain independence in the western hemisphere (and second only after the United States) came Haiti, violently, in 1804. After the second world war, Britain freed its West Indian islands (with a few exceptions) after having planted the seeds of parliamentary democracy. Unlike in tormented Haiti, these seeds have flourished: the ex-British West Indies offers a shining example of respect for freedom and human rights on small islands with fragile economies. Their challenge is economic: to adapt their agriculture and grow fruits and vegetables where they have a comparative advantage (unlike bananas, where they do not).

Many influences

The dominant influences, cultures and languages in Latin America have been Spanish and Portuguese; but not entirely. When this book was being written, the president of Argentina was of Syrian origin, the president of Peru was an ethnic Japanese, the president of Paraguay had Hungarian ancestors, the president of Chile had some British blood and the president of El Salvador had Italian roots. Millions of poor but enterprising Europeans have sailed over the past century and a half to Latin America in the hope of making a fortune. Some succeeded, especially in Argentina, Venezuela and Brazil.

The dominant outsiders

Until independence under Simon Bolivar beginning in 1819, Latin America was run by Spanish and Portuguese colonial administrations. They were by all accounts fairly easy-going if you were Spanish, less so if you were American Indian. There was no hint of democracy. Viceroys listened, if they were intelligent, to the advice of the local Spanish oligarchs. Bolivar's revolution, which enjoyed some surreptitious and effective help from Britain (aiming to reduce the influence in Europe of Spain), and the subsequent collapse of Portuguese power in Brazil, left a vacuum. In an act of bravado by the leader of a young and weak state, President James Monroe of the United States enunciated in 1823 what was to be known as the Monroe Doctrine: "The American continents, by the free and independent condition which they have assumed and maintained, are henceforth not to be considered as subjects for colonisation by any European powers." President Monroe pledged that the United States would help any Latin American country whose sovereignty was threatened by nations from outside the hemisphere. Latin American critics came to see the doctrine as a charter for meddling in their internal affairs.

First came the British

The vacuum was mostly filled by tough British businessmen in Argentina, Uruguay, Brazil, Bolivia and Mexico, but there was no spiritual or sentimental affinity. The language was an impediment (as it still is today). However, the British built much of the infrastructure in the region including railways and public utilities. British influence lasted roughly until the second world war. Before it, Mexico nationalised Britain's oil interests; after it, Venezuela did so. In post-war Argentina, President Peron nationalised the British-run railways. As the British empire shrivelled worldwide, so did Britain's influence over Latin America. The other powerful influence was – and is – the United States.

Uncle Sam takes over

In a series of military interventions in the 1920s and 1930s, the United States took power temporarily in several small Caribbean countries whose governments had not paid their debts. It took over the Customs and Excise and collected enough American money to pay off the arrears. In the case of Nicaragua, marines also presided over the country's first genuinely free presidential election since independence. (Unfortunately, the man it brought to power became a puppet in the hands of the national guard commander, Anastasio Somoza, who swiftly became a dictator.) American interventions were extremely unpopular. President Roosevelt laid the groundwork for a more benevolent attitude with his "Good Neighbour" policy in which he undertook to treat Latin America seriously and to consult with its leaders. He was not above a touch of jocular cynicism, however. "He may be a bastard," Roosevelt is quoted as saying of Somoza, "but he's our bastard."

Ike played tough

Under President Eisenhower and the brothers John Foster and Allen Dulles, secretary of state and director of the CIA respectively, the United States took a cold-war interest in Latin America. In Guatemala, deploying a great deal of bluff, a CIA-backed ragtag band of rebels in the countryside with a portable radio transmitter scared the leftist president, Jacobo Arbenz, into fleeing to Cuba in 1954. After Fidel Castro had expropriated all American property in Cuba without compensation, adopted hardline communist tactics and gained the habit of throwing crude and gratuitous insults at the United States in his long and rambling speeches, Eisenhower imposed an embargo on American trade with the island in 1961. He approved preparations for an invasion of Cuba by exiles, trained by the Americans in Guatemala. (The plan, inherited and approved by President Kennedy, failed when he refused at the last minute to provide the invasion with American air cover.)

The need for change

Kennedy was the first American president to recognise the need for social justice in Latin America and the danger of leaving unjust societies to fester. He offered American aid through his "Alliance for Progress", launched in 1961. Up to 1970 when it began to fade, the alliance directed foreign aid and government-to-government co-operation to democratically elected presidents such as Romulo Betancourt in Venezuela, Janio Quadros in Brazil, Arturo Frondizi in Argentina, Fernando Belaunde in Peru, Eduardo Frei in Chile and Alberto Lleras Camargo and Carlos Lleras Restrepo in Colombia. Democracy visited Central America briefly in the same period, represented by Ramon Villeda Morales in Honduras and Juan Jose Arevalo in Guatemala (the predecessor of Arbenz) while Costa Rica enjoyed a stream of democratically elected presidents.

A new generation

At the same time Latin America was changing. The well-to-do sent their children increasingly to American universities. The graduates returned home full of ambition, wanting to help their countries to modernise and catch up with America's democracy, its rate of economic growth and its evident prosperity. Air-conditioning replaced roof fans and people worked harder; old attitudes began to fade. But not among the generals, who still thought civilian politicians could not be trusted and that only they could run their country honestly and competently. The democratic optimism of the Alliance for Progress in the 1960s gave way to "national-security" military regimes, determined to stamp out any hint of Castroite guerrilla warfare. The army took over in Brazil from 1964 until 1985; Argentina from 1966 until 1984 (with one interruption); Peru from 1968 to 1980; Uruguay from 1973 to 1984; Chile from 1973 to 1989; and in Bolivia almost permanently. The generals also dominated Guatemala, Honduras, Panama and El Salvador while the Somoza dictatorship ruled Nicaragua.

Powerless people

This was a dark era for Latin America. Murder and torture of "subversives" was widespread in Chile, Argentina, Brazil and Uruguay. Ordinary people felt no responsibility for their country or their society; government was taken out of their hands by a military power, sometimes cruel or wilful or corrupt, that could not be challenged except by guerrilla warfare, which it was. Guerrillas trained and armed with weapons or just with encouraging words in Havana fought, killed, kidnapped and detonated explosives in most parts of the region. These young men and women were, like the young graduates from American colleges, determined to break with the past and make their country a better place. They thought it could be done through Marxism. They had the opportunity to try out their theory in Bolivia, where the flamboyant Argentine revolutionary, Ernesto "Che" Guevara, having abandoned a high position in Castro's Cuba, tried to organise a peasants' revolt. But the peasants, all smallholders, roundly rejected him, and he was caught and killed by the army in 1967. In Nicaragua the Sandinist guerrillas took power. But their revolution failed and they lost the free elections that they were obliged to hold.

Change in the Church

Refecting Latin American society, the Church was split. On one side were the traditionalists, mostly elderly senior clerics who took the view that the priest's principal tasks were to celebrate mass and care for the souls of his parishioners. Very often priests were sympathetic to the landed gentry who held the power in their parishes. To the left of the traditionalists were the reformists, believers who sought to create a better world by working in Christian Democratic parties such as Chile's, Venezuela's or El Salvador's. One such reformist was Chile's President Eduardo Frei. To the left of the reformists were the advocates of "liberation theology", radical young priests working in desperately poor parishes who endorsed Marxism and the concept of class warfare and violence, with the Church firmly on the side of the oppressed. The viscerally anti-communist Pope John Paul, who visited the region regularly, advocated a middle course. Priests should give preference to the needs of the poor, he said. But they should also be "poles of unity" in their communities.

Prebisch predominates

At the same time a new view of economic development gained ground. It was propounded by Raul Prebisch, executive secretary of the UN's Economic Commission for Latin America. Prebisch argued in favour of high-tariff protectionism of Latin America's infant industries, giving them a headstart against international competition in order to produce substitutes for imported goods. He was not enthusiastic about encouraging exports or foreign investment. He railed against the world's unjust terms of trade. Many governments adopted his ideas in one form or another. At one level, protectionism works. It enables companies to establish themselves behind tariff walls, creates jobs and reduces the need to use valuable foreign-exchange reserves on imports. After the infant industries are properly set up, the high tariff walls should theoretically be dismantled. But they stayed high. The protected companies became inefficient in a stagnant market. They did not export because they were not internationally competitive.

Happy 70s, miserable 80s

True to their long history of improvident fiscal policies, governments – military ones to the forefront – borrowed heavily on the world market in the 1970s to cover their current-account deficits or to build ambitious projects. Western commercial banks, in their unwisdom, chose to pump billions of dollars of their investors' deposits into government bonds printed by Latin American governments. These enabled the region to record a modest level of economic growth in the 1970s based on other people's money. But the debts began to pile up. The crunch came in 1982 when Mexico could not service its foreign debt of some $100 billion. Interested governments and banks rushed to its rescue and a crisis of international banking confidence was avoided. But it soon became clear that Latin America, not just Mexico, could not service its debts.

The fireman arrives

This time the United States did not send in the marines. Instead an extraordinary co-operative effort was launched to seize the opportunity that the crisis offered. Debtor countries had to work out agreements with the International Monetary Fund under which they would obtain loans in return for "letters of intent" promising economic good behaviour. This meant cutting budget deficits and inflation; freeing exchange rates; opening up markets to competition from imports while encouraging exports; and inviting foreign investments. These policies were backed by the World Bank. The commercial banks agreed to reschedule the debt (delay repayment of capital). This worked well, as far as it went. But it left a lot of governments with precious little foreign exchange in their reserves. They needed to borrow some more to help them through their sticky patch. One attempt to help was called the "Baker Plan" after the American treasury secretary, James Baker. He urged the banks to lend "new money" to governments which carried out all the right reforms. The plan failed because the banks, badly burnt by the debt crisis, did not produce "new money" for the Latin Americans.

The system works, more or less

Nonetheless, slowly and very painfully, the reforms were applied. Governments became unpopular. Budget cuts meant cuts in government services such as schools, hospitals and subsidies intended for the poor. The banks abruptly cut off Latin America from any new money. As a result there was a massive capital outflow as the Latin Americans paid interest on their vast debts. GDP fell almost everywhere. The 1980s were later called the "lost decade". The name was wrong. It was the region's most productive decade in this century. New economic policies began to work. Budget cuts reduced inflation. Import tariffs, formerly 100% or more, came down to 30%, 20% and sometimes even 10%. Import licences, and the accompanying bribery, were abolished. Multiple exchange rates, and opportunities for making fast millions on the money market, were abolished too.

A dramatic shake-up

Some companies forced to compete with cheap imports found they could do so and even export as well. Others failed. Overall, non-traditional exports boomed. Loss-making state-owned companies were sold off in a wave of privatisations that reached its peak in the early 1990s. Some were swapped for foreign-debt certificates bought on the unofficial market at a cut rate but honoured by the debtor government at the full rate. The cash was released by the government in local currency and only for an agreed purchase of a stake in a company to be privatised. These "debt-for-equity swaps" were a dramatic success. Debt paper, sold on the secondary market, had in the case of some countries sunk in value to 10 cents per dollar. As the reforms took effect and the economic recovery began, the value of the debt paper of most countries shot up.

The "Brady Plan"

At the same time, it was increasingly realised that agreements to reschedule foreign debts helped by delaying capital repayments but left unsolved the massive "debt overhang" on which interest had to be paid. This was dealt with in debt-reduction agreements along lines suggested by Mr Baker's successor as American treasury secretary, Nicholas Brady. Creditor banks were given the options of selling their debt paper at a loss (35% in some cases) and pulling out of a debtor country, or staying on new terms. These terms could include the option of keeping the original amount of debt but with a much lower rate of interest or accepting a reduced debt at the standard interest rate. There was also an option to lend "new money". The IMF provided valuable help. "Brady Plan" agreements gave Latin American countries an important psychological boost.

A surprising bonus

With Chile in the forefront, national economies began to grow again. Chile gave its economy a boost by privatising pensions and telling pension funds to invest their money in the stockmarket. They did, and it woke up. Sleepy stockmarkets in other countries woke up too. For entirely extraneous reasons, the Latin Americans were given a helping hand by the United States. Anxious to pull the country out of recession, President Bush and the Federal Reserve pushed interest rates down as far as they would go. This had two beneficial effects: it slashed the interest bill that Latin Americans had to pay on their foreign debt and it encouraged Latin Americans who had salted their money away in Miami or New York to bring it home, where interest rates were much higher. This strengthened foreign-exchange reserves. Sometimes the return of "flight capital" was too much to handle and risked provoking inflation.

Back to barracks

The regional economic crisis badly tarnished the reputation of the ruling generals in several countries, and they thought it wise to retreat. With the concerted help of elected Latin American presidents, Ronald Reagan and West European leaders, country after country went democratic. Between 1980 and 1992 the generals stepped down in Brazil, Argentina, Uruguay, Paraguay, Chile, Peru, Ecuador, Honduras, Guatemala and El Salvador. In Nicaragua the dictatorship was overthrown by left-wing Sandinists whose own authoritarian regime was defeated at the polls. In Panama the drug-running military boss, Manuel Noriega, was removed by the United States. Mexico's almost-one-party regime was beginning to hold clean state and local elections and promising clean presidential ones. By 1994 there were only two fully fledged dictatorships left: Cuba's and Haiti's.

Rebirth-pangs

Democracy could not have chosen a worse time to return. Most civilian presidents took over economic crises and had to apply austerity programmes. To their lasting credit, most of them did not shrink from doing so. In many cases, ruling parties were ousted in the first available election by dissatisfied voters. But the policies continued and power was transferred peacefully from ruling party to opposition party. Since the 1980s this important test of a new or reborn democracy has been passed by Argentina, Brazil, Chile, Peru, Bolivia, Honduras, Guatemala and El Salvador.

Elected Latin American leaders began to enjoy meeting each other at innumerable "summits" unnoticed by the rest of the world. Each of these meetings was a reaffirmation of regional democracy. With their new openness to the world, the Latin Americans decided to be more open to each other. Thus Argentina, Brazil, Uruguay and Paraguay formed their "southern market" (Mercosur), designed to become a free-trade area. Colombia and Venezuela established a free-trade area that became a roaring success and was joined by Ecuador. Guatemala, El Salvador and Honduras started a free-trade area with the hope of attracting more foreign investment. Chile signed up for free trade with Mexico and Colombia, and Colombia in turn signed up with Mexico and the Central Americans. All were stirred by, and had their eyes on, Mexico's admission to the North American Free Trade Agreement. The island states of the former British West Indies formed the 12-member Caribbean Community (Caricom) and by 1994 all but two had approved a common external tariff.

The next priorities

Having established both democracy and free-market policies aimed at sustained, non-inflationary, export-led growth, what next is in store for Latin America? The new policies, efficiently applied, ought to provide what all Latin Americans want: more jobs after a painful period when inefficient firms laid off unneeded workers. Beyond that, demand will grow for something simple but hard to achieve: good government. This means decent old-age pensions; unemployment insurance; honest police and judges; well-run hospitals; an efficient telephone service; reliable water supply; proper sewage treatment; docks and airports which handle freight competently; honest supervisors of privatised public utilities; and above all better public education. If Latin America is to compete, its people must be better educated. The danger is that the gap between rich and poor will grow, that Latin America will become a penthouse built on a slum. By one reckoning there are 40m "street children" in Latin America heading for an adult life of crime. Already many Latin American cities suffer from crime waves. Now that they are supported by more or less sound economies, Latin American governments and socio-economic elites must face the urgent need to provide social justice for their peoples.

Part I

COUNTRY RANKINGS

18 Size and society
Area
Population
Population growth
Population density
Youngest populations
Human development index

20 Living standards
Life expectancy: men
Life expectancy: women
Infant mortality
Doctors and patients
Literacy
People per telephone
People per TV

22 The economy
GDP
GDP per head
Purchasing power
GDP change
Agriculture's contribution to GDP
Inflation
Debt
Debt as % of GDP
Debt service

Size and society

Area *sq km*

1	Brazil	8,511,965	16	Cuba	110,860
2	Argentina	2,766,890	17	Guatemala	108,890
3	Mexico	1,972,201	18	French Guiana	91,000
4	Peru	1,285,216	19	Panama	78,200
5	Colombia	1,138,914	20	Costa Rica	51,100
6	Bolivia	1,098,580	21	Dominican Republic	48,730
7	Venezuela	912,050	22	Haiti	27,750
8	Chile	756,945	23	Belize	22,960
9	Paraguay	406,750	24	El Salvador	21,040
10	Ecuador	283,560	25	Bahamas	13,940
11	Guyana	214,970	26	Jamaica	10,990
12	Uruguay	176,220	27	Puerto Rico	9,104
13	Suriname	163,270	28	Trinidad & Tobago	5,130
14	Nicaragua	129,494	29	Guadeloupe	1,780
15	Honduras	112,090	30	Martinique	1,100

Population *millions*

1	Brazil	156.8	16	Paraguay	4.5
2	Mexico	85.0	17	Nicaragua	4.1
3	Colombia	33.4	18	Puerto Rico	3.6
4	Argentina	33.1	19	Costa Rica	3.1
5	Peru	22.3		Uruguay	3.1
6	Venezuela	20.3	21	Jamaica	2.5
7	Chile	13.6		Panama	2.5
8	Cuba	10.8	23	Trinidad & Tobago	1.3
9	Ecuador	10.7	24	Guyana	0.8
10	Guatemala	9.7	25	Martinique	0.4
11	Bolivia	7.8		Suriname	0.4
12	Dominican Republic	7.5	27	Bahamas	0.3
13	Haiti	6.8		Barbados	0.3
14	Honduras	5.5	29	Belize	0.2
15	El Salvador	5.4		Netherlands Antilles	0.2

Population growth *average annual growth 1987–92, %*

1	Nicaragua	3.4		Mexico	2.0
2	Belize	3.3		Panama	2.0
3	Honduras	3.2	18	Suriname	1.9
4	Antigua & Barbuda	3.1	19	Bahamas	1.6
5	Bolivia	2.9		Chile	1.6
	Guatemala	2.9	21	El Salvador	1.3
	Paraguay	2.9	22	Argentina	1.2
8	Colombia	2.4	23	Martinique	1.1
	Ecuador	2.4	24	Cuba	1.0
	Venezuela	2.4		Jamaica	1.0
11	Costa Rica	2.2	26	Puerto Rico	0.9
	Dominican Republic	2.2	27	Barbados	0.8
13	Peru	2.1		Trinidad & Tobago	0.8
14	Brazil	2.0	29	Uruguay	0.6
	Haiti	2.0	30	Guyana	0.5

Population density *population per sq km*

1	Bermuda	1200	16	St. Kitts & Nevis	149
2	Barbados	605	17	Cayman Islands	112
3	Puerto Rico	393	18	Montserrat	100
4	Martinique	336	19	Cuba	98
5	St. Vincent & Grenadines	324	20	Dominica	93
6	Aruba	311	21	Guatemala	89
7	Virgin Islands (US)	281	22	Anguilla	76
8	El Salvador	257	23	Costa Rica	61
9	Grenada	246	24	Honduras	49
	Trinidad & Tobago	246	25	Mexico	48
11	Haiti	244	26	Ecuador	38
12	Jamaica	225	27	Nicaragua	32
13	Netherlands Antilles	177		Panama	32
14	Antigua & Barbuda	159	29	Colombia	31
15	Dominican Republic	153	30	Turks & Caicos	30

Youngest populations *% aged under 15*

1	Nicaragua	45.9	16	Peru	35.5
2	Guatemala	45.2		Suriname	35.5
3	Honduras	44.8	18	Brazil	35.4
4	El Salvador	43.7	19	Grenada	35.2
5	Bolivia	42.5	20	Panama	34.9
6	Belize	41.4	21	Venezuela	34.7
7	St Lucia	41.3	22	Guyana	34.6
8	Paraguay	41.1		St. Vincent & Grenadines	34.6
9	Haiti	40.0	24	Jamaica	34.2
10	Ecuador	39.5	25	Trinidad & Tobago	33.9
11	Antigua & Barbuda	38.0	26	Montserrat	33.3
12	Dominica	37.5	27	Colombia	32.9
13	Dominican Republic	37.3	28	Bahamas	31.8
14	Costa Rica	36.1	29	Chile	30.4
15	Mexico	36.0	30	St. Kitts & Nevis	30.0

Human development index

1	Barbados	92.8	17	Brazil	73.0
2	Uruguay	88.1	18	St Lucia	72.0
3	Trinidad & Tobago	87.7	19	Cuba	71.1
4	Bahamas	87.5	20	St. Vincent & Grenadines	70.9
5	Chile	86.4	21	St. Kitts & Nevis	69.7
6	Costa Rica	85.2	22	Belize	68.9
7	Argentina	83.2	23	Ecuador	64.6
8	Venezuela	82.4	24	Paraguay	64.1
9	Dominica	81.9	25	Peru	59.2
10	Mexico	80.5	26	Dominican Republic	58.6
11	Grenada	78.7	27	Guyana	54.1
12	Antigua	78.5	28	El Salvador	50.3
13	Colombia	77.0	29	Nicaragua	50.0
14	Suriname	75.1	30	Guatemala	48.9
15	Panama	73.8	31	Honduras	47.2
16	Jamaica	73.6			

Living standards

Life expectancy: men *age in years*

1	Costa Rica	75		Mexico	67
2	Cuba	74		Venezuela	67
3	Panama	73	16	Colombia	66
4	Jamaica	72		Dominican Republic	66
5	Paraguay	71		Guyana	66
6	Puerto Rico	70		Suriname	66
7	Chile	69	20	Honduras	65
	Uruguay	69	21	Brazil	64
9	Argentina	68	22	Peru	63
	El Salvador	68	23	Guatemala	61
	Trinidad & Tobago	68	24	Nicaragua	60
12	Belize	67	25	Bolivia	59
	Ecuador	67	26	Haiti	53

Life expectancy: women *age in years*

1	Costa Rica	79		Trinidad & Tobago	73
	Cuba	79	15	Colombia	72
	Puerto Rico	78		Ecuador	72
4	Panama	77	17	Guyana	71
5	Chile	76		Suriname	71
	Jamaica	76	19	Dominican Republic	70
	Uruguay	76	20	Brazil	69
8	Argentina	75	21	Honduras	68
	El Salvador	75	22	Guatemala	66
10	Paraguay	74		Nicaragua	66
	Mexico	74		Peru	66
	Venezuela	74	25	Bolivia	64
13	Belize	73	26	Haiti	55

Infant mortality *number of deaths per 1,000 live births*

1	Haiti	104		Mexico	30
2	Bolivia	82	15	Paraguay	28
3	Brazil	67	16	El Salvador	26
4	Peru	59	17	Uruguay	23
5	Nicaragua	57		Venezuela	23
6	Dominican Republic	56	19	Jamaica	18
	Guatemala	56	20	Chile	17
8	Honduras	54		Panama	17
9	Ecuador	42		Trinidad & Tobago	17
10	Guyana	36	23	Puerto Rico	14
11	Argentina	34	24	Costa Rica	12
	Suriname	34	25	Cuba	11
13	Belize	30			

a 1991.

Doctors and patients *number of people per doctor*[a]

1	Argentina	370	13	Mexico	1,240
2	Uruguay	510	14	Suriname	1,260
3	Cuba	530	15	Paraguay	1,460
4	Venezuela	700	16	Honduras	1,510
5	Ecuador	820	17	Bolivia	1,530
6	Trinidad & Tobago	940	18	Nicaragua	1,560
7	Costa Rica	960	19	Dominican Republic	1,770
8	Panama	1,000	20	Jamaica	2,040
9	Peru	1,040	21	Guatemala	2,180
10	Brazil	1,080	22	Belize	2,220
11	Chile	1,160	23	El Salvador	2,830
12	Colombia	1,230	24	Haiti	7,140

Literacy *% of adult population*[a]

1	Guyana	98	12	Panama	88
2	Jamaica	98		Venezuela	88
3	Uruguay	96	14	Colombia	87
4	Argentina	95		Mexico	87
	Suriname	95	16	Ecuador	86
6	Cuba	94	17	Peru	85
7	Chile	93	18	Dominican Republic	83
	Costa Rica	93	19	Brazil	81
9	Paraguay	90	20	Bolivia	78
	Puerto Rico	90	21	El Salvador	73
11	Nicaragua	88		Honduras	73

Number of people per telephone[a]

1	Haiti	111.1	11	Colombia	12.3
2	Honduras	71.4	12	Venezuela	10.9
3	Guatemala	62.5	13	Brazil	10.4
4	Paraguay	37.0		Mexico	10.4
5	El Salvador	37.0	15	Suriname	9.9
6	Bolivia	34.5	16	Panama	9.6
7	Peru	32.3	17	Argentina	8.7
8	Ecuador	27.8	18	Costa Rica	7.0
9	Cuba	19.2	19	Uruguay	6.1
10	Chile	14.7	20	Trinidad & Tobago	5.7

Number of people per TV[a]

1	Haiti	200.0	13	Mexico	7.2
2	Guatemala	19.2	14	Costa Rica	6.7
3	Paraguay	16.9	15	Panama	6.1
4	Nicaragua	16.1	16	Belize	6.0
5	Honduras	13.9		Venezuela	6.0
6	Ecuador	12.0	18	Chile	4.9
7	Dominican Republic	11.9	19	Cuba	4.8
8	El Salvador	11.1	20	Brazil	4.7
9	Peru	10.3	21	Argentina	4.5
10	Colombia	8.7	22	Uruguay	4.3
11	Jamaica	7.7	23	Trinidad & Tobago	3.3
	Suriname	7.7			

The economy

GDP *$bn*

1	Brazil	424.0	16	Panama	6.1
2	Mexico	294.8	17	Paraguay	6.0
3	Argentina	200.3	18	Bolivia	5.1
4	Venezuela	58.9	19	Trinidad & Tobago	5.0
5	Colombia	44.6	20	Bahamas	3.2
6	Chile	37.1		Jamaica	3.2
7	Puerto Rico	23.6	22	Honduras	3.1
8	Peru	21.3	23	Haiti	2.5
9	Cuba	20.3	24	Barbados	1.7
10	Ecuador	11.8		Suriname	1.7
11	Uruguay	10.4	26	Nicaragua	1.3
12	Guatemala	9.6		Netherlands Antilles	1.3
13	Dominican Republic	7.6	28	Aruba	1.1
14	Costa Rica	6.3	29	Cayman Islands	0.6
	El Salvador	6.3	30	St Lucia	0.5

GDP per head *$*

1	Cayman Islands	18,137	17	St Lucia	2,900
2	Aruba	15,674		Venezuela	2,900
3	Bahamas	12,020	19	Brazil	2,760
4	Netherlands Antilles	7,058	20	Chile	2,730
5	Puerto Rico	6,610	21	Dominica	2,520
6	Barbados	6,530	22	Panama	2,440
7	Turks & Caicos	6,413	23	Grenada	2,310
8	Argentina	6,050	24	Belize	2,210
9	Anguilla	5,652	25	Costa Rica	2,000
10	Montserrat	4,886	26	Cuba	1,880
11	Antigua	4,870	27	St. Vincent & Grenadines	1,655
12	St. Kitts & Nevis	3,990	28	Paraguay	1,340
13	Trinidad & Tobago	3,940		Jamaica	1,340
14	Suriname	3,700	30	Colombia	1,330
15	Mexico	3,470	31	El Salvador	1,170
16	Uruguay	3,340			

Purchasing power *GDP per head in PPP (USA=100)*[a]

1	Puerto Rico	49.3	12	Ecuador	18.7
2	Trinidad & Tobago	37.9	13	Jamaica	16.6
3	Venezuela	36.7	14	Paraguay	15.5
4	Mexico	32.4	15	Guatemala	14.4
5	Chile	31.9	16	Peru	14.1
6	Uruguay	30.1	17	Dominican Republic	13.9
7	Colombia	24.7	18	Nicaragua	11.5
8	Brazil	23.7	19	Bolivia	9.8
9	Argentina	23.1	20	El Salvador	9.5
10	Costa Rica	23.0	21	Honduras	8.2
11	Panama	22.2	22	Haiti	5.5

a 1991.

GDP change *annual average % change, 1987–92*

1	Belize	7.9	15	Mexico	3.1
2	Chile	7.3		Dominican Republic	3.1
3	St. Vincent & Grenadines	6.4	17	El Salvador	2.9
4	St. Kitts & Nevis	5.3	18	Uruguay	2.5
5	Antigua & Barbuda	4.7	19	Argentina	1.7
6	Costa Rica	4.4	20	Bahamas	1.3
	Ecuador	4.4	21	Panama	0.9
8	Venezuela	4.2	22	Guyana	0.6
9	Guatemala	3.9	23	Suriname	0.5
	Grenada	3.9	24	Brazil	-0.1
11	Bolivia	3.6	25	Barbados	-1.0
	Honduras	3.6	26	Nicaragua	-2.7
	Dominica	3.6	27	Peru	-5.0
14	Colombia	3.5			

Agriculture's contribution to GDP %[a]

1	Guyana	50	16	El Salvador	10
2	Nicaragua	30		Uruguay	10
3	Bolivia	29		Panama	10
4	Dominica	26	19	Chile	9
	Guatemala	26	20	Mexico	7
6	Honduras	22		Peru	7
	Paraguay	22	22	Argentina	6
8	Belize	21		Venezuela	6
9	Costa Rica	18	24	Bahamas	5
	Dominican Republic	18		Barbados	5
11	Colombia	16		Jamaica	5
12	Cuba	15	27	Anguilla	4
	Ecuador	15		Montserrat	4
14	Grenada	14	29	Trinidad & Tobago	3
15	Brazil	11			

Inflation *average annual rate of increase, 1988–93, %*

1	Argentina	1504.0	8	Colombia	28.1
2	Brazil	736.0	9	Costa Rica	19.0
3	Peru	460.0	10	Mexico	18.8
4	Uruguay	82.2	11	Chile	18.5
5	Ecuador	54.1	12	Honduras	16.9
6	Venezuela	44.6	13	Bolivia	14.7
7	Dominican Republic	40.0	14	Trinidad & Tobago	10.0

Foreign debt

Debt *$bn*

1	Brazil	121.1	13	Dominican Republic	4.6
2	Mexico	113.4	14	Jamaica	4.3
3	Argentina	67.6	15	Bolivia	4.2
4	Venezuela	37.2	16	Costa Rica	4.0
5	Peru	20.3	17	Honduras	3.6
6	Chile	19.4	18	Guatemala	2.7
7	Colombia	17.2	19	Trinidad & Tobago	2.3
8	Ecuador	12.3	20	El Salvador	2.1
9	Nicaragua	11.1	21	Paraguay	1.7
10	Puerto Rico	10.0	22	Haiti	0.8
11	Panama	6.5	23	Belize	0.2
12	Uruguay	5.3			

Debt as % of GDP

1	Nicaragua	822.6	13	Uruguay	46.8
2	Guyana	501.0	14	Trinidad & Tobago	46.0
3	Jamaica	153.6	15	Puerto Rico	40.3
4	Honduras	114.2	16	Belize	38.5
5	Panama	111.8	17	Colombia	36.7
6	Ecuador	102.1	18	Mexico	35.2
7	Peru	95.4	19	El Salvador	33.4
8	Bolivia	83.6	20	Brazil	31.3
9	Costa Rica	63.2	21	Argentina	30.1
10	Venezuela	62.5	22	Haiti	28.8
11	Dominican Republic	61.9	23	Paraguay	27.8
12	Chile	49.3	24	Guatemala	26.8

Debt service ratio[a]

1	Mexico	44.4	12	Trinidad & Tobago	25.2
2	Paraguay	40.9	13	Jamaica	24.8
3	Bolivia	39.1	14	Peru	23.0
4	Colombia	35.3	15	Uruguay	22.2
5	Honduras	35.0	16	Chile	20.9
6	Argentina	34.9	17	Costa Rica	20.7
7	Brazil	31.3	18	Venezuela	19.5
	Panama	31.3	19	Dominican Republic	13.5
9	Guatemala	28.1	20	El Salvador	13.3
10	Ecuador	27.1	21	Haiti	6.6
11	Nicaragua	26.5			

a Debt service consists of interest payments on outstanding debt plus any principal repayments due. The debt service ratio is debt service expressed as a percentage of a country's earnings from exports of goods and services.

Part II

CENTRAL AMERICA COUNTRY PROFILES

26 Belize
30 Costa Rica
34 El Salvador
38 Guatemala
42 Honduras
46 Mexico
52 Nicaragua
56 Panama

BELIZE

Total area	22,960 sq km	Population	200,000
GDP	$442m	GDP per head	$2,210
Capital	Belmopan	Other cities	Belize City

English-speaking Belize is a small Central American country with a tiny population and a colourful people. Spanish colonial rule did not reach across the mostly empty flatlands on the Caribbean coast, so the area was populated by British pirates and traders as well as runaway slaves and their children, Mayan Indians, Black Carib Indians known as *garufana*, *creoles* (people of mixed race partly descended from blacks) and *mestizos* (people of mixed American Indian and European blood). Belize is a sleepy place, well off the beaten track. It is, however, beginning to wake up.

History: claim and counter-claim

Spain recognised British sovereignty of what became known as British Honduras in 1802 but after gaining their independence from Spain both Mexico and Guatemala laid claim to the territory. The Mexicans soon dropped theirs and Guatemala recognised British sovereignty in 1859 in return for a British promise to build a road from Guatemala City to the Caribbean coast. But Britain did not keep its promise. Guatemala did not take up the issue until 1945 when it abrogated the treaty. The dispute persisted and sporadic discussions were held at the United Nations, with Britain insisting on its territorial rights in the sure knowledge that the inhabitants had no desire to be ruled by a Guatemalan dictator. In response to bellicose talk from Guatemala City, a small force of Harrier jump-jet ground-attack aircraft was stationed at Belize City airport and the territory received regular visits from a British frigate that became known as the Belize guardship.

Independence came late

In 1973 the territory was renamed Belize and eight years later it attained independence despite Guatemalan protests. George Price, leader of the People's United Party, became prime minister. After a democratic government took over in Guatemala in 1986, hopes were raised that it would at last recognise Belizean independence. But President Vinicio Cerezo, who re-opened negotiations, stopped short of that. Agreement finally came in 1991 under Mr Cerezo's successor, Jorge Serrano. In 1994 the jump-jets began to leave, a battalion of British soldiers was reduced to a company and some jungle camps were abandoned.

Politics: dozing in the sun

Under Mr Price Belize became a stable democracy. However, ignored by a world more interested in wars and rebellions, it decayed quietly. Mr Price was occasionally accused by his critics of being over-friendly with Cuba's President Castro and the Sandinist regime in Nicaragua. In 1984 he lost a general election (and his own seat) to the opposition United Democratic Party of Manuel Esquivel, a pro-American and pro-business politician. The voters turned against Mr Esquivel in 1989 and put Mr Price back in office. But in a snap election four years later they turned back to Mr Esquivel.

Society: immigrants and drugs

By one reckoning some 30,000 people have settled in Belize from elsewhere in the region, especially El Salvador. This influx amounts to about 15% of the population and it has strained the government's limited services. There has not, however, been any outbreak of resentment among Belizeans against the newcomers. There is fear that increasing numbers of Colombian drug-traffickers are using landing strips in Belize since the downfall of Panama's dictator, Manuel Noriega, meant they could no longer stop off in Panama. The traffickers are believed to launder some of their money by buying legitimate enterprises in Belize and to pay off their Belize employees in cocaine rather than money. There is a danger – so far nothing more – that this small and essentially defenceless community may be corrupted.

The economy: Belize wakes up

The basis of the economy is agriculture, tourism and remittances from abroad. At first timber dominated. Then came sugar (now declining), oranges, bananas, mangoes and pineapples and – more recently – lobsters, shrimps and textiles. An export processing zone has been opened at San Andres. American investors realised that here was a friendly, stable country on good terms with their government and less than two hours from Miami. Hotels sprang up on the beautiful and unspoilt coast in places like Ambergris Cay, which is ideal for fishing.

Total area	22,960 sq km	Highest point metres	Victoria Peak 1,112
Capital	Belmopan		
Other cities	Belize City	Main rivers	Sarstoon, Belize

The economy

GDP $m	442	GDP per head $	2,210
% av. ann. growth in real GDP 1987–92	7.9	GDP per head in purchasing power parity (USA=100)	...

Origins of GDP	*% of total*	**Components of GDP**	*% of total*
Agriculture	21	Private consumption	64
Industry	36	Public consumption	19
of which:		Investment	30
manufacturing	17	Exports	69
Services	43	Imports	-83

Structure of manufacturing

% of total

Agric. & food processing	...	Other	...
Textiles & clothing	...	Av. ann. increase in industrial output 1987–92	...
Machinery & transport	...		

Inflation and exchange rates

Consumer price 1992 av. ann. incr.	2.8%	Belize $ per $ av. 1993	2.00
Av. ann. rate 1987–92	3.3%	Belize $ per ecu av. 1993	2.24

Balance of payments, reserves, aid and debt

$bn

Visible exports fob	0.1	Capital balance	0.03
Visible imports fob	-0.2	Overall balance	nil
Trade balance	-0.1	Change in reserves	nil
Invisible inflows	0.1	Level of reserves end Dec.	0.05
Invisible outflows	-0.1	Foreign debt	0.2
Net transfers	0.02	as % of GDP	38.5
Current account balance	-0.04	Debt service	
as % of GDP	-8.3	as % of export earnings	...

Principal exports	*$m fob*	**Principal imports**	*$m cif*
Sugar	38	Food	49
Citrus concentrate	27	Machinery	48
Garments	16	Fuels	33
Fish products	12	Chemicals	25

Main export destinations	*% of total*	**Main origins of imports**	*% of total*
USA	48.6	USA	56.6
UK	27.3	UK	8.5
Mexico	3.2	Mexico	8.8
Canada	3.1	Canada	2.0

Government

System Constitutional monarchy and parliamentary democracy with governor-general representing Queen Elizabeth II. Bicameral National Assembly comprising 28-member House of Representatives and 11-member Senate.

Main political parties People's United Party, United Democratic Party

Climate and topography

Tropical. Very hot and humid with rainy season from May to February. Flat swampy coastal plain with low mountains in south.

People and society

Population	200,000	% under 15	41.4
Pop. per sq km	9	% over 65	4.3
% urban	50	No. men per 100 women	100
% av. ann. growth 1987–92	3.3	Human Development Index	68.9
No. households m	92		

Life expectancy	*yrs*	**Education**	
Men	67	Spending as % of GDP	...
Women	73	Years of compulsory education	...
Crude birth rate	31	Adult literacy %	...
Crude death rate	5	Primary school enrolment %	...
Infant mortality		Secondary school enrolment %	...
per 1,000 live births	30	Tertiary education enrolment %	...

Workforce	*% of total*	**Consumer goods ownership**	
Services	...		*Pop. per*
Industry	...	Car	...
Agriculture	...	TV	6.0
% unemployed	...	Telephone	...

Ethnic groups	*% of total*	**Religious groups**	*% of total*
Creole	40	Roman Catholic	62
Mestizo	33	Anglican	12
Maya	10	Methodist	6
Garifuna	8	Mennonite	4
East Indian	2	Seventh-Day Adventist	3

Tourism		**Health**	
Tourist arrivals m	0.2	Pop. per doctor	2,220
Tourist receipts $bn	0.1		

COSTA RICA

Total area	51,100 sq km	Population	3.1m
GDP	$6.3bn	GDP per head	$2,000
Capital	San Jose	Other cities	Alajuela, Limon, Cartago

Costa Rica is a model for all Latin American and all developing countries. It is small and without oil or minerals. Yet good government since 1948 has given it a national health service and old-age pensions, one of the highest literacy rates in the world and free university education. It has no army. Costa Rica has pursued mostly free-market policies that have given the country an atmosphere of social justice and civil peace.

History: roots of success

Costa Rica (rich coast) belied its name. The Spanish *conquistadores* found no gold there. The land had only a tiny population of migrant American Indians. It was settled by poor yeoman farmers who developed an independent-minded spirit. There were no big estates and all-powerful bosses. The system of land tenure almost guaranteed that Costa Rica would become democratic. After independence from Spain in 1821 and the usual post-independence political turmoil, the country embraced democracy in 1889. Apart from a coup and counter-coup in 1917 and a dramatic turnabout in 1948, the country has remained democratic and stable.

Politics: the events of 1948

The result of the presidential election in 1948 was annulled after the government's candidate, Rafael Calderon, who came second, refused to accept defeat. An opposition leader, Jose Figueres, led a revolt in favour of the winning candidate, Otilio Ulate. An interim regime was set up, the constitution was changed, the army was abolished and Mr Ulate became president. Mr Figueres succeeded him in the election of 1953. With the help of the reformist bishop of San Jose, the capital, and a communist union leader, he began to push through social reforms.

Peace and progress

Mr Figueres, a democratic socialist, was president twice (1953–58 and 1970–74). As leader of the National Liberation Party (PLN) the diminutive "Don Pepe" exercised strong influence. His power was counter-balanced by the conservative Social Christian Unity Party, which claimed it would roll back the PLN's socialist excesses. The upshot was an economy with large private and state sectors.

Trouble next door

Costa Rica looks down its nose at its impoverished and heavily *mestizo* neighbour to the north, Nicaragua. But it also did its best to help the country solve its problems and thus deter a heavy inflow of Nicaraguan immigrants. Under President Rodrigo Carazo, Costa Rica was a conduit for arms from Cuba to the Nicaraguan Sandinist rebels fighting the hated dictator, Anastasio Somoza. The Cuban consul in San Jose, a key intelligence officer, handled the operation. Some Costa Rican officials are said to have enriched themselves. After the Sandinists won, and began to impose a leftist pro-Cuban regime, democratic Costa Rica changed its mind and helped anti-Sandinist rebels such as Eden Pastora ("Commander Zero"). Eventually President Oscar Arias (1986–90) master-minded Nicaraguan peace negotiations. The anti-Sandinist rebels were disarmed in return for ironclad Sandinist guarantees to hold a free general election. The Sandinists kept their promise and lost. Mr Arias was awarded the Nobel Peace Prize.

The economy: big spenders

Some governments lived beyond their means. They borrowed money abroad or printed it at home. Costa Rica acquired a foreign debt and inflation. President Carazo bequeathed to his successor, Luis Alberto Monge, an economy with inflation at 120% and a budget deficit amounting to 14% of GDP. Mr Monge had to spend much of his presidency picking up the pieces. In 1982 his deflationary policies led to a 7.5% drop in GDP. Mr Arias's preoccupation with being a regional statesman led him to neglect the economy. It was under his conservative successor, Rafael Angel Calderon (son of the man who caused the trouble in 1948), that a serious effort was made to cut down the budget deficit and the role of the state. The budget deficit fell from 4.4% of GDP in 1990, Mr Arias's last year, to 1% in 1993.

Inflation fell from 25% in 1991 to 9% in 1993. GDP increased from 3.4% in 1990 to 6.8% in 1992 and 6% in 1993. The country's main worry in 1994, apart from restrictions on banana exports to the European Union, was a rapid increase in the current-account deficit. But overall Costa Rica was making steady progress and dreaming of joining the United States, Canada and Mexico in the North American Free Trade Agreement.

Total area	51,100 sq km	% agricultural area	58
Capital	San José	Highest point metres	Chirripo Grande 3,819
Other cities	Alajuela, Limon, Cartago	Main rivers	Reventazon, San Juan

The economy

GDP $bn	6.3	GDP per head $	2,000
% av. ann. growth in real GDP 1987–92	4.4	GDP per head in purchasing power parity (USA=100)	23.0

Origins of GDP	*% of total*	**Components of GDP**	*% of total*
Agriculture	18	Private consumption	61
Industry	25	Public consumption	16
of which:		Investment	23
manufacturing	...	Exports	39
Services	56	Imports	-46

Structure of manufacturing

			% of total
Agric. & food processing	47	Other	39
Textiles & clothing	8	Av. ann. increase in industrial	
Machinery & transport	6	output 1987–92	...

Inflation and exchange rates

Consumer price 1993 av. ann. incr.	9.8%	Colones per $ av. 1993	142.2
Av. ann. rate 1987–93	19.0%	Colones per ecu av. 1993	159.3

Balance of payments, reserves, aid and debt

			$bn
Visible exports fob	1.7	Capital balance	0.3
Visible imports fob	-2.2	Overall balance	0.03
Trade balance	-0.5	Change in reserves	0.1
Invisible inflows	0.9	Level of reserves end Dec.	1.0
Invisible outflows	-1.0	Foreign debt	4.0
Net transfers	0.09	as % of GDP	63.2
Current account balance	-0.4	Debt service	
as % of GDP	-5.7	as % of export earnings	20.7

Principal exports	*$m fob*	**Principal imports**	*$m cif*
Bananas	533	Intermediate goods	983
Coffee	203	Consumer goods	644
Beef	67	Capital goods	559
		Construction materials	86

Main export destinations	*% of total*	**Main origins of imports**	*% of total*
USA	55.2	USA	53.6
Germany	7.5	Japan	6.7
Italy	5.0	Venezuela	4.6
Canada	3.4	Mexico	3.6

Government

System Democratic republic. President and two vice-presidents elected for 4-year terms. Unicameral legislative assembly. Establishment of an army forbidden by constitution.

Main political parties National Liberation Party, Social Christian Unity Party

Climate and topography

Tropical with rainy season from May to November. Coastal plains separated by rugged mountains.

People and society

Population m	3.1	% under 15	36.1
Pop. per sq km	61	% over 65	4.2
% urban	47	No. men per 100 women	102
% av. ann. growth 1987–92	2.2	Human Development Index	85.2
No. households m	...		

Life expectancy	*yrs*	**Education**	
Men	75	Spending as % of GDP	4.6
Women	79	Years of compulsory education	6
Crude birth rate	27	Adult literacy %	93
Crude death rate	4	Primary school enrolment %	87
Infant mortality		Secondary school enrolment %	42
per 1,000 live births	12	Tertiary education enrolment %	26

Workforce	*% of total*	**Consumer goods ownership**	
Services	46		*Pop. per*
Industry	30	Car	18.9
Agriculture	24	TV	6.7
% unemployed	4.3	Telephone	7.0

Ethnic groups	*% of total*	**Religious groups**	*% of total*
White	96	Roman Catholic	95
Black	2		
Indian	1		
Chinese	1		

Tourism		**Health**	
Tourist arrivals m	0.4	Pop. per doctor	960
Tourist receipts $bn	0.3		

EL SALVADOR

Total area	21,040 sq km	Population	5.4m
GDP	$6.3bn	GDP per head	$1,170
Capital	San Salvador	Other cities	Santa Ana, San Miguel

El Salvador is the smallest country in Central America and the most densely populated. Its people are among the most hard-working and enterprising. But the majority are poor and hungry for land or jobs or both. Although there has been some reform, much of the land remains in the hands of a small class of medium-sized farmers. For many years El Salvador was torn apart by a civil war. It is now at peace and has a chance to fulfil its potential.

History: repression and exploitation

After independence from Spain in 1823, El Salvador was ruled directly or indirectly by the leading landowners, all of Spanish origin. The presidency changed hands within a select group of rivals. Only the forms of democracy were respected. The indigenous population became farm labourers, sometimes with a small plot of land. The first protest of any size came in 1931, when a reformist, Arturo Araujo, was elected president. The ruling elite, worried about the communists led by Farabundo Marti, allowed General Maximiliano Hernandez Martinez to take over. The next year he put down a peasant revolt. As many as 30,000 people may have been killed; Marti was one of the victims. The country remained pacified until 1970, ruled by generals and occasionally civilians who won the presidency either by coups or rigged elections. Trade unions and other left-wing organisations were banned.

Politics: the man in the middle

Social injustice bred a communist revolution led by the Farabundo Marti National Liberation Front (FMLN) which for decades murdered its perceived enemies (such as elected mayors, town councillors and government officials) and laid waste the infrastructure (including the country's main bridge). At the other extreme were a scared and occasionally brutal army and vicious paramilitary death squads, ready to kill presumed leftists, union leaders and other "subversives" and dump their bodies in a ravine outside the capital. In the civilised centre was the key figure in El Salvador's modern history, Jose Napoleon Duarte, a Christian Democrat. Duarte at first joined a government with reformist generals, in 1980, that nationalised the banks and foreign trade in coffee and cotton, the country's main exports, then in the hands of powerful interests.

This junta also paved the way for a free presidential election which Duarte won. Political discourse became reasoned rather than violent. The rebels and the death squads carried on, but Duarte's efforts to respect human rights undermined the hard men of the left and the right. Duarte's flaw was that, while being an honest man himself, he allowed himself to be surrounded by men who were less scrupulous. His conservative successor, Federico Cristiani of the opposition Nationalist Republican Alliance, signed a peace agreement with the rebels in the presence of the UN secretary-general, Javier Perez de Cuellar, in 1992. Although President Cristiani came from the party led at one stage by Roberto d'Aubuisson, who was widely suspected of having close contacts with the death squads, he charted a moderate course. The peace accord provided for the dismantling of the rebel army and its absorption into civil life and politics. In 1992 the FMLN formed its own political party. In 1994 Armando Calderon Sol, the candidate of Mr Cristiani's party, won the presidential election with the FMLN candidate taking second place.

Society: mixed and lively

The majority of the population, of mixed American Indian and European blood, is poor and under-privileged but very enterprising. Under Duarte thousands of tenant smallholders were able to obtain title to the land they tilled (a reform that worked) and many big estates were taken over by cooperatives (a reform that did not work).

The economy: cautious hopes

Under Mr Cristiani plans were made to privatise the nationalised banks and cotton and coffee export agencies, which did not prove efficient. The exchange rate became competitive. In 1991 the old dream of a common market with neighbouring Guatemala and, possibly, the rest of Central America, took shape. This 19th century idea was tried in the 1960s without success. A limited deal with Guatemala and Honduras which was designed to deepen and widen to include the rest of Central America was approved. But the country still depended too much on exports of coffee and cotton, for which world prices in the early 1990s were low. But democracy was being consolidated. El Salvador should approach its goal of political and economic stability for the first time in decades.

Total area	21,040 sq km	% agricultural area	54
Capital	San Salvador	Highest point metres	Santa Ana
Other cities	Santa Ana,		2,381
	San Miguel	Main rivers	Lempa

The economy

GDP $bn	6.3	GDP per head $	1,170
% av. ann. growth in		GDP per head in purchasing	
real GDP 1987–92	2.9	power parity (USA=100)	9.5

Origins of GDP	*% of total*	**Components of GDP**	*% of total*
Agriculture	10	Private consumption	88
Industry	24	Public consumption	11
of which:		Investment	14
manufacturing	19	Exports	15
Services	66	Imports	-29

Structure of manufacturing

			% of total
Agric. & food processing	...	Other	...
Textiles & clothing	...	Av. ann. increase in industrial	
Machinery & transport	...	output 1987–92	...

Inflation and exchange rates

Consumer price 1992 av. ann. incr.	11.2%	Colones per $ av. 1993	8.67
Av. ann. rate 1987–92	17.3%	Colones per ecu av. 1993	9.71

Balance of payments[a], reserves, aid and debt

			$bn
Visible exports fob	0.6	Capital balance	-0.06
Visible imports fob	-1.3	Overall balance	-0.1
Trade balance	-0.7	Change in reserves	-0.1
Invisible inflows	0.3	Level of reserves end Dec.	0.4
Invisible outflows	-0.5	Foreign debt	2.1
Net transfers	0.5	as % of GDP	33.4
Current account balance	-0.2	Debt service	
as % of GDP	-2.3	as % of export earnings	13.3

Principal exports	*$m fob*	**Principal imports**	*$m cif*
Coffee	225	Raw materials &	
Textiles & garments	79	intermediate goods	825
Sugar	31	Capital goods	565
Shrimp	26	Consumer goods	522
		Building materials	141

Main export destinations	*% of total*	**Main origins of imports**	*% of total*
USA	29.9	USA	44.2
Guatemala	22.0	Guatemala	10.8
Costa Rica	9.0	Mexico	5.9
Honduras	6.5	Japan	5.1

Government

System Republic with president elected for non-renewable term of 5 years. Unicameral legislative assembly elected for a term of 3 years.

Main political parties National Republican Alliance, Christian Democratic Party, Farabundo Marti National Liberation Front (FMLN)

Climate and topography

Tropical with rainy season from May to October. Mostly mountains with narrow coastal belt and central plateau.

People and society

Population m	5.4	% under 15	43.7
Pop. per sq km	257	% over 65	3.6
% urban	44	No. men per 100 women	96
% av. ann. growth 1987–92	1.3	Human Development Index	50.3
No. households m	...		

Life expectancy	*yrs*	**Education**	
Men	68	Spending as % of GDP	1.8
Women	75	Years of compulsory education	8
Crude birth rate	33	Adult literacy %	73
Crude death rate	5	Primary school enrolment %	70
Infant mortality		Secondary school enrolment %	26
per 1,000 live births	26	Tertiary education enrolment %	17

Workforce	*% of total*	**Consumer goods ownership**	
			Pop. per
Services	55		
Industry	35	Car	35.7
Agriculture	10	TV	11.1
% unemployed	9	Telephone	37.0

Ethnic groups	*% of total*	**Religious groups**	*% of total*
Mestizo	89	Roman Catholic	75
Indian	10	Protestant	25
White	1		

Tourism		**Health**	
Tourist arrivals m	0.2	Pop. per doctor	2,830
Tourist receipts $m	69		

a 1991.

GUATEMALA

Total area	108,890 sq km	Population	9.7m
GDP	$9.6bn	GDP per head	$980
Capital	Guatemala City	Other cities	Puerto Barrios, Quezaltenango

Guatemala is a small country with a long history of violence that springs in part from the chasm between rich and poor and from long years of military misrule. Unexpectedly, however, Guatemala has held two consecutive free elections and removed a president from office constitutionally. The level of violence is diminishing.

History: a bleak house

Since independence from Spain in 1821 Guatemala has been mostly ruled by generals or their friends. The longest such period was the presidency of General Jorge Ubico (1931–44), who closed the country to foreign influence. He was succeeded by a freely elected and popular president, Juan Jose Arevalo (1945–51), who tried to establish the rule of law and promote social justice. As a consequence he had to survive several coup attempts. He handed over to his elected successor, Colonel Jacobo Arbenz, a leftist who tried to break up the big estates. He was seen by the elite and the American ambassador to be a communist. After a coup manipulated by the CIA in 1954, he went to live in Cuba.

The era of the generals

Colonel Arbenz was succeeded by another colonel, Carlos Castillo Armas, who thought the best communist was a dead one and was himself killed in 1957. Next came a succession of generals and civilian front-men who provoked the growth of several guerrilla groups. The worst general was Romeo Lucas Garcia (1978–82), under whose government at least 11,000 supposed guerrillas or subversives were said to have been killed in 1981 alone. Torture was commonplace. Thousands fled to Mexico. Mr Garcia was succeeded by a popular born-again Protestant reformer, General Efrain Rios Montt, who tried to fight corruption, reform the judiciary and disband the secret police. He launched a programme of giving "rifles and beans" to Indians who did not support the guerrillas. (By 1994 there were only a few hundred guerrillas left, and they were negotiating for peace.)

Politics: a brighter moment

The election of 1985 was won by the Christian Democratic candidate, Vinicio Cerezo Arevalo, a nephew of Juan Jose Arevalo, who had spent much of his life in fear of being detained, tortured and murdered. Mr Arevalo introduced free-market reforms and tried to stop the killings. In the second half of his presidency he let public spending slip out of control. He achieved his ambition of ending his mandate without incident. But there were several attempted coups and numerous murders of teachers, trade-unionists and others perceived by right-wing extremists to be "subversives". His successor was Jorge Serrano, a centrist with ties to the business community. Exasperated by obstruction and corruption in Congress, Mr Serrano tried to seize near-dictatorial powers in May 1993 but won no support. He was voted out of office and replaced by the respected human-rights ombudsman, Ramiro de Leon Carpio, who immediately became enmeshed in a campaign to oblige the unpopular Congress and the Supreme Court (both widely viewed as corrupt) to resign. An election was due in August 1994.

Society: divided

Guatemalan society has three layers. The bottom layer, which is the biggest, comprises poor American Indians, who speak their own languages, have their own culture and wear their own colourful clothes. They live in the "Mayan Highlands" in the centre of the country, where they often eke out a living on small and over-cultivated plots of land. Many have left for the cities, where they wear western clothes. The second, thinner layer is of better-off mixed-blood *ladinos* who live in towns and cities. The thinnest layer comprises the well-to-do modern farmers of the lowlands and businessmen in Guatemala City led by 28 powerful families. The Indians, men in particular, need to keep their pride in their roots and self-respect. This is difficult in a Hispanic-dominated society.

Economy: Serrano tries reforms

Mr Cerezo bequeathed a near-bankrupt, inflationary economy to Mr Serrano, who briskly put it in order. He cut inflation and the economy began to grow (by 4% in 1993). He promoted the free-trade area including El Salvador and Honduras. Guatemala's traditional exports amounted in 1992 to about $215m, consisting of coffee, sugar, bananas, cardamom, meat and cotton. Non-traditional exports, including shrimp, exotic vegetables such as snow peas and textiles accounted for $170m in 1992. A modest industrial base has been built up. Mr de Leon Carpio tried resolutely to improve tax collection in order to spend more on the poor but found it difficult.

Total area	108,890 sq km	% agricultural area	28
Capital	Guatemala City	Highest point metres	Tajumulso
Other cities	Puerto Barrios,		4,220
	Quezaltenango	Main rivers	Coyolate, Motagua

The economy

GDP $bn	9.6	GDP per head $	980
% av. ann. growth in real GDP 1987–92	3.9	GDP per head in purchasing power parity (USA=100)	14.4

Origins of GDP	*% of total*	**Components of GDP**	*% of total*
Agriculture	26	Private consumption	84
Industry	20	Public consumption	6
of which:		Investment	14
manufacturing	...	Exports	18
Services	55	Imports	-24

Structure of manufacturing

			% of total
Agric. & food processing	43	Other	44
Textiles & clothing	9	Av. ann. increase in industrial	
Machinery & transport	3	output 1987–92	...

Inflation and exchange rates

Consumer price 1992 av. ann. incr.	10.1%	Quetzal per $ av. 1993	5.63
Av. ann. rate 1987–92	20.6%	Quetzal per ecu av. 1993	6.31

Balance of payments, reserves, aid and debt

			$bn
Visible exports fob	1.3	Capital balance	0.6
Visible imports fob	-2.3	Overall balance	-0.01
Trade balance	-1.0	Change in reserves	-0.05
Invisible inflows	0.7	Level of reserves end Dec.	0.8
Invisible outflows	-0.7	Foreign debt	2.7
Net transfers	0.3	as % of GDP	26.8
Current account balance	-0.7	Debt service	
as % of GDP	-6.8	as % of export earnings	28.1

Principal exports	*$m fob*	**Principal imports**	*$m cif*
Coffee	267	Raw materials &	
Sugar	143	intermediate goods	978
Bananas	98	Capital goods	695
Tobacco	40	Consumer goods	677
		Fuel	200

Main export destinations	*% of total*	**Main origins of imports**	*% of total*
USA	37.3	USA	45.1
El Salvador	14.3	Mexico	6.5
Costa Rica	7.1	El Salvador	5.3
Honduras	5.7	Japan	5.3

Government

System Republic with president directly elected for 5-year term. Unicameral legislative assembly comprises 100 members.
Main political parties National Centrist Union, Solidarity Action Movement, Christian Democratic Party

Climate and topography

Tropical. Hot and humid in lowlands, cooler in highlands. Mostly mountains with narrow coastal plains and rolling limestone plateau.

People and society

Population m	9.7	% under 15	45.2
Pop. per sq km	89	% over 65	3.0
% urban	39	No. men per 100 women	101
% av. ann. growth 1987–92	2.9	Human Development Index	48.9
No. households m	...		

Life expectancy	*yrs*	**Education**	
Men	61	Spending as % of GDP	...
Women	66	Years of compulsory education	...
Crude birth rate	34	Adult literacy %	55
Crude death rate	8	Primary school enrolment %	...
Infant mortality		Secondary school enrolment %	21
per 1,000 live births	56	Tertiary education enrolment %	9

Workforce	*% of total*	**Consumer goods ownership**	
			Pop. per
Services	29		
Industry	23	Car	...
Agriculture	48	TV	19.2
% unemployed	6.1	Telephone	62.5

Ethnic groups	*% of total*	**Religious groups**	*% of total*
Ladino	56	Roman Catholic	95
Indian	44		

Tourism		**Health**	
Tourist arrivals m	0.5	Pop. per doctor	2,180
Tourist receipts $bn	0.2		

HONDURAS

Total area	112,090 sq km	Population	5.5m
GDP	$3.1bn	GDP per head	$580
Capital	Tegucigalpa	Other cities	San Pedro Sula

Poor and under-developed, Honduras has been mostly ruled by generals. It has been heavily influenced by American banana companies and been called the quintessential banana republic. Its public services, roads and ports are inadequate. However, Honduras may at last be pulling itself up by its bootstraps.

History: Morazan started it

After independence from Spain in 1821, Honduras with other Central American provinces formed a government of the United Provinces of Central America. The second president was a young military leader from Honduras, Francisco Morazan, who pushed through liberal reforms. He was, however, ousted by an illiterate conservative leader in 1840. Thereafter Honduras was ruled by a military and civilian elite in Tegucigalpa, the capital. Illiterate peasants, engaged in subsistence farming, had no say at all.

Politics: a taste of democracy

Genuine democracy came briefly when Ramon Villeda Morales, a popular, moderate reformist and a Liberal, won a free election in 1957. But he was ousted by a general in 1963 and military rule continued until 1980. In 1969 a "soccer war" was set off by disorders after two World Cup qualifying matches between Honduras and El Salvador. The root cause, however, was discontent over the number of Salvadorans who had moved across the border and over a territorial dispute. The "war" ended in a truce. In 1992 the two sides accepted a World Court ruling.

The politicians return

Honduras held free elections again in 1980 and the Liberal Roberto Suazo, a wily but lazy country doctor, won. He allowed the army chief, General Adolfo Alvarez, to become the most powerful man in the country. Younger officers packed him off to Miami. Dr Suazo was succeeded by Jose Azcona (1986–91), a Liberal who was resolute in his denials of the well-known existence on Honduran soil of American-backed Nicaraguan "contra" rebels. Mr Azcona supported the contras because he thought they were fighting the "communist" Sandinist regime (and their presence brought millions of dollars to Honduras). Mr Azcona was succeeded by Rafael Callejas of the National Party. Mr Callejas, a graduate of Louisiana State University, proved to be one of the "new men" of Latin America: a vigorous, free-market, reformist democrat. His reforms were successful but also painful, and in the 1993 presidential election the voters turned to a Liberal, Carlos Reina.

Society: a long way to catch up

For centuries Honduras has been a sleepy backwater. Only in the 1990s has the challenge of widespread poverty, illiteracy and ill health been faced. Lacking funds, and being unwilling to resort to the printing press, successive governments have had little impact.

The economy: finally, a shake-up

In the late 19th and early 20th centuries vast tracts of land were sold off to American companies, particularly the United Fruit Company. This was not a case of wicked imperialism as its critics claimed: the company invested where nobody had bothered to invest before, employed thousands of workers and provided a modicum of medical care, unlike some Honduran landowners. But its power was excessive.

Mr Callejas slashed import tariffs and export taxes, extracted the country from a financial crisis, established good relations with the IMF and World Bank, devalued and stabilised the currency and set the country finally on the road to stable, non-inflationary, export-led growth. He brought Honduras into a common market to be worked out with El Salvador and Guatemala. GDP growth went from 0.1% in 1990 to about 2% in 1991 and 3.5% in 1992 and 1993. Inflation fell from 10.5% in 1989 to 6.5% in 1992. It was a considerable achievement.

Exports have an uneven record. Agriculture depends on bananas (involved in a dispute over entry to the European market), coffee (hurt by low world prices) and cattle-raising (doing well). Non-traditional exports such as prawns, pineapples, melons and zinc are expanding. Export-processing zones are attracting investors. But the country still runs a trade deficit. Mr Callejas was anxious to provide a "safety net" for the poorest of the poor but Honduras itself is among the poorest of the poor countries and has little to spare for social welfare. It will take a long time for the Honduran economy to take off. However, this fragile light aircraft has started to move in the direction of the runway.

Total area	112,090 sq km	% agricultural area	46
Capital	Tegucigalpa	Highest point metres	
Other cities	San Pedro Sula,	Main rivers	Patuca, Ulvia, Guayape

The economy

GDP $bn	3.1	GDP per head $	580
% av. ann. growth in real GDP 1987–92	3.6	GDP per head in purchasing power parity (USA=100)	8.2

Origins of GDP	*% of total*	**Components of GDP**	*% of total*
Agriculture	22	Private consumption	70
Industry	27	Public consumption	10
of which:		Investment	24
manufacturing	16	Exports	31
Services	51	Imports	-10

Structure of manufacturing

			% of total
Agric. & food processing	51	Other	38
Textiles & clothing	9	Av. ann. increase in industrial	
Machinery & transport	2	output 1987–92	...

Inflation and exchange rates

Consumer price 1993 av. ann. incr.	10.7%	Lempiras per $ av. 1993	5.83
Av. ann. rate 1987–93	16.9%	Lempiras per ecu av. 1993	6.53

Balance of payments, reserves, aid and debt

			$bn
Visible exports fob	0.8	Capital balance	-0.01
Visible imports fob	-1.0	Overall balance	-0.3
Trade balance	-0.2	Change in reserves	0.1
Invisible inflows	0.3	Level of reserves end Dec.	0.2
Invisible outflows	-0.6	Foreign debt	3.6
Net transfers	0.06	as % of GDP	114.2
Current account balance	-0.3	Debt service	
as % of GDP	-9.6	as % of export earnings	35.0

Principal exports	*$m fob*	**Principal imports**'	*$m cif*
Bananas	287	Industrial supplies	369
Coffee	148	Consumer goods	250
Lobsters & prawns	97	Capital goods	215
Zinc	37	Fuels & lubricants	162

Main export destinations	*% of total*	**Main origins of imports**	*% of total*
USA	52.4	USA	54.2
Germany	14.3	Mexico	6.6
Italy	5.1	Guatemala	4.7
Belgium-Luxembourg	4.8	Panama	4.0

Government

System Republic with strongly presidential system. President is elected for 4-year term. Members of unicameral National Congress elected on proportional basis.

Main political parties Liberal Party, National Party

Climate and topography

Sub-tropical in lowlands, temperate in mountains. Mostly mountains in interior with narrow coastal plains.

People and society

Population m	5.5	% under 15	44.8
Pop. per sq km	49	% over 65	3.1
% urban	44	No. men per 100 women	102
% av. ann. growth 1987–92	3.2	Human Development Index	47.2
No. households m	...		

Life expectancy	*yrs*	**Education**	
Men	65	Spending as % of GDP	4.6
Women	68	Years of compulsory education	6
Crude birth rate	37	Adult literacy %	73
Crude death rate	7	Primary school enrolment %	91
Infant mortality		Secondary school enrolment %	32
per 1,000 live births	54	Tertiary education enrolment %	9

Workforce	*% of total*	**Consumer goods ownership**	
			Pop. per
Services	47		
Industry	17	Car	111.1
Agriculture	36	TV	13.9
% unemployed	6.4	Telephone	71.4

Ethnic groups	*% of total*	**Religious groups**	*% of total*
Mestizo	90	Roman Catholic	97
Indian	7		
Black	2		
White	1		

Tourism		**Health**	
Tourist arrivals m	0.2	Pop. per doctor	1,510
Tourist receipts $m	2.9		

a 1990.

MEXICO

Total area	1,972,201 sq km	Population	85m
GDP	$294.8bn	GDP per head	$3,470
Capital	Mexico City	Other cities	Guadalajara, Monterrey

Mexico is going through a transformation that may with continued good judgment set it on a road to fast economic growth, as a partner of the United States and Canada in the North American Free Trade Agreement (NAFTA), and multi-party democracy. But more than half the population still live in poverty. Their misery will be alleviated by economic growth and a better distribution of the country's wealth.

History: unhappy memories

After hundreds of years of rule by Aztecs, Mayas, Zapotecs, Olmecs, Totomacs, Toltecs and other cultures, Mexico was discovered by the Spaniard, Hernan Cortes, in 1519. Cortes beguiled and controlled the Aztec ruler, Montezuma, and defeated his son, Cuauhtemoc, in a battle on a lake close to Mexico City. The original Mexicans became virtual slaves to their new rulers, who plundered the land, built churches on the ruins of temples that they had destroyed and invested little. After independence from Spain in 1821, Mexico was ruled mostly by generals, notably Agustin de Iturbide and Antonio de Santa Ana. In 1847 Mexico lost a border war with the United States and in a settlement ceded much of what is now the south-western United States.

Civil war

From 1858 to 1860 Mexicans fought in a civil war between anti-clerical reformists led by a Zapotec lawyer, Benito Juarez, and pro-church conservatives. Juarez became the first indigenous president. But in 1861 the government could not service its debt. Creditor countries – France, Britain and Spain – sent a ground force aboard gunboats. The French ventured as far as Puebla, where they were beaten by Juarez's men. Two years later they seized Mexico City. In a bizarre episode, Louis Napoleon installed the Archduke Maximilian of Habsburg as emperor of Mexico. The French withdrew but a few months later the Mexicans rose again. Maximilian was captured at Queretaro and shot by firing squad. Juarez, who had disregarded appeals from European leaders to show mercy, resumed the presidency.

Exploiter and moderniser?

In 1876 General Porfirio Diaz took power and was to hold it for 35 years. Diaz has been reviled as a tool of British and

American exploiters who enriched themselves at the expense of the poor Mexicans. But the investors also began to modernise Mexico. The oil industry was launched by the British. Banks, railways and mines were started. By 1910, however, Mexicans felt the need for social justice.

A sticks-and-stones revolution

In 1910 the revolution erupted. Much of it was a struggle for power between rival leaders with their own armies: Francisco Madero, Venustiano Carranza and Alvaro Obregon, the peasant leader, Emiliano Zapata, and the ruthless Pancho Villa. Order was restored during the two presidential terms of the astute, anti-clerical Plutarco Elias Calles (1924–28). It was, however, only under General Lazaro Cardenas (1934–40) that government institutions were consolidated. Cardenas nationalised the oil industry. He launched a system of 180,000 farming co-operatives called *ejidos* over 46m acres. He formed the National Peasant Confederation to give the peasantry a voice within the ruling party. Unions were formed and linked to the party, which became identified with the Mexican version of a corporate state. It won every election.

President Miguel Aleman (1946–52), who left office worth, it was claimed, $60m, renamed the ruling Mexican Revolutionary Party as the Institutional Revolutionary Party (PRI). The new name neatly summed it up. But the "institution" was decaying. The free-spending President Jose Lopez Portillo (1976–82) left office in disgrace having brought Mexico to the point where it could not service its foreign debt and having destroyed business confidence by nationalising the banks.

The new Mexico

His successor, Miguel de la Madrid (1982–88), did not mind imposing austerity and being unpopular. He cut the fiscal deficit from about 15% of GDP to zero, purged ministries, started to privatise the state sector, cut import tariffs to make local industry more competitive, joined the GATT and made the exchange rate competitive. He worked out debt-assistance packages with commercial-bank creditors, the IMF and the World Bank. Inflation was brought under control with a pact on wage and price restraint with labour and management. Mexico became somewhat more democratic: elections were less obviously rigged and opposition voices began to be heard more clearly. Mr de la Madrid was one of the country's great presidents. He was, however, unloved: average earnings fell by roughly 40% in six years.

Politics: a thoroughly modern president

Mr de la Madrid was succeeded by Carlos Salinas de Gortari, scion of a well-to-do political family who obtained his doctorate at Harvard. In second place was Cuauhtemoc Cardenas, son of Lazaro, who had been a prominent member of the PRI and broken with it over the reforms. Mr Cardenas headed a left-wing electoral alliance including communists calling for a return to subsidies, state intervention, tariff protection and anti-American nationalism. In third place, representing free-market, libertarian conservatives, was Manuel Clouthier of the National Action Party (PAN), which had for decades attacked the PRI as the representative of a corrupt corporate state. Mr de la Madrid and Mr Salinas stole the PAN's best clothes. Mr Cardenas claimed he had been robbed of the presidency. Opposition parties made gains in Congress, which came to life for the first time in living memory.

Faster still

Mr Salinas raced ahead. He privatised the banks, the telephone company, an airline, a steelworks and countless other state enterprises. He launched a programme of building toll highways and ran a fiscal policy which balanced the budget and helped bring inflation down to 9%. He called for primary elections for offices in the states. He rescinded some PRI victories in state elections following claims that they had been rigged. But the PRI headquarters in Mexico City still comprises two tall office buildings. The big television network Televisa is entirely pro-PRI; so are most newspapers and many radio stations. Some reporters are paid off by the ministries they cover. The PRI's candidate to succeed Mr Salinas was Luis Donaldo Colosio, a former president of the PRI, later minister for social affairs and administrator of the president's "Solidarity" programme, a fast-disbursing (and therefore popular) public-works scheme. Mr Colosio was assassinated during the presidential election campaign and replaced as the PRI candidate by the less colourful but intelligent and tough Ernesto Zedillo.

Foreign policy: a new approach

Mr Salinas's foreign policy represented a U-turn from the long-standing line of maintaining Mexico's "identity" by keeping a distance from the United States. Mr Salinas struck up a good working relationship with Presidents Bush and Clinton. He became a partner with infinitely more input on American policy than any of his predecessors. Without this relationship, NAFTA could not have been negotiated; the prickly problem of dealing with cross-border drug-trafficking would have been much more difficult.

Society: uneven development

The 20th century has provided Mexicans with roads, electricity and water supply and, for many, sewage and telephone services as well as a modest level of education. This is the achievement of the PRI. But the urban and rural poor, many of them American Indians, struggle for survival. In his budget for 1993 Mr Salinas allocated 60% of expenditure to health, education and other social services. The seemingly unbridgeable gap between rich and poor led desperate landless peasants in the remote southern state of Chiapas to rebel in January 1994. The thoroughly modern men in Mexico City, who had thought the country was doing well, were astonished. Peace negotiations produced promises by the government to make election procedures, dominated by the PRI, open to closer independent supervision.

The economy: big gains, high risks

NAFTA will make Mexico attractive to foreign investors as a low-wage coun'ry with tariff-free access to the United States. A sustained capital inflow is needed because the country has been running a current-account deficit (in 1993 it was $21 billion). However, inflation in 1993 crossed the psychological barrier of two figures (from 12% in 1992 to 9% in 1993). There were some notable weaknesses. GDP growth was slipping: from 4.4% in 1990 to 3.6% in 1991, 2.6% in 1992 and 1% in 1993 (lower than the rate of population growth). The trade deficit was also discouraging: $11.3 billion in 1991, $20.6 billion in 1992 and $19.5 billion in 1993. The foreign debt, no longer treated as a worry, was creeping up to $125 billion in 1993. However, another important signal was positive: foreign-exchange reserves (minus gold) increased from $5.6 billion in 1986 to $18.9 billion in December 1993. Some of this arrived as so-called "hot money" to be invested in Mexican bonds, because interest rates were higher than in the United States, or the stockmarket and could be pulled out quickly if needed. But much of the foreign-exchange inflow took the form of capital investments. These in turn led in many cases to imports of capital goods, thereby adding to the trade deficit. Mexico's rulers could count on the prospect that the economy would grow steadily. The world of politics looked more volatile.

Total area	1,972,201 sq km	% agricultural area	52
Capital	Mexico City	Highest point metres	Orizaba 5,700
Other cities	Guadalajara, Monterrey	Main rivers	Grande, Balsas

The economy

GDP $bn	294.8	GDP per head $	3,470
% av. ann. growth in real GDP 1987–92	3.1	GDP per head in purchasing power parity (USA=100)	32.4

Origins of GDP	*% of total*	Components of GDP	*% of total*
Agriculture	7	Private consumption	68
Industry	33	Public consumption	11
of which:		Investment	21
manufacturing	23	Exports	18
Services	60	Imports	-18

Structure of manufacturing

			% of total
Agric. & food processing	22	Other	54
Textiles & clothing	15	Av. ann. increase in industrial	
Machinery & transport	9	output 1987–92	4.0

Inflation and exchange rates

Consumer price 1993 av. ann. incr.	9.7%	New pesos per $ av. 1993	3.16
Av. ann. rate 1987–93	18.8%	New pesos per ecu av. 1993	3.54

Balance of payments, reserves, aid and debt

			$bn
Visible exports fob	27.5	Capital balance	26.4
Visible imports fob	-48.2	Overall balance	1.7
Trade balance	-20.7	Change in reserves	1.9
Invisible inflows	17.0	Level of reserves end Dec.	18.9
Invisible outflows	-21.5	Foreign debt	113.4
Net transfers	2.4	as % of GDP	35.2
Current account balance	-22.8	Debt service	
as % of GDP	-7.7	as % of export earnings	44.4

Principal exports	*$bn fob*	Principal imports	*$bn cif*
Manufactured goods	35.2	Intermediate goods	42.8
Oil & oil products	8.3	Capital goods	11.6
Agricultural products	2.1	Consumer goods	7.7

Main export destinations	*% of total*	Main origins of imports	*% of total*
USA	68.7	USA	65.2
Spain	4.4	Japan	6.3
Japan	3.2	Germany	5.1
Canada	2.8	France	2.7
France	2.0	Italy	2.3

Government

System Federal republic comprising 31 states and a federal district. President is elected directly. Bicameral National Congress consisting of Senate and Chamber of Deputies.

Main political parties Institutional Revolutionary Party, National Action Party, Democratic Revolutionary Party

Climate and topography

Varies by terrain and latitude, extending from arid deserts with extreme temperatures to humid tropical climates. High, rugged mountains, low coastal plains, high plateaus and deserts.

People and society

Population m	85	% under 15	36.0
Pop. per sq km	48	% over 65	4.0
% urban	73	No. men per 100 women	99
% av. ann. growth 1987–92	2.0	Human Development Index	80.5
No. households m	...		

Life expectancy	*yrs*	**Education**	
Men	67	Spending as % of GDP	4.1
Women	74	Years of compulsory education	9
Crude birth rate	29	Adult literacy %	87
Crude death rate	5	Primary school enrolment %	98
Infant mortality		Secondary school enrolment %	53
per 1,000 live births	30	Tertiary education enrolment %	14

Workforce	*% of total*	**Consumer goods ownership**	
			Pop. per
Services	47		
Industry	31	Car	15.4
Agriculture	22	TV	7.2
% unemployed	3.2	Telephone	10.4

Ethnic groups	*% of total*	**Religious groups**	*% of total*
Mestizo	60	Roman Catholic	89
Indian	30	Protestant	6
White	9		

Tourism		**Health**	
Tourist arrivals m	6.4	Pop. per doctor	1,240
Tourist receipts $bn	5.3		

NICARAGUA

Total area	129,494 sq km	Population	4.1m
GDP	\$1.3bn	GDP per head	\$410
Capital	Managua	Other cities	Leon

Nicaragua has a tormented history of dictatorship, greed, brutality and corruption plus devastating earthquakes. By one reckoning about 60% of the workforce is unemployed. The poverty is deep and desperate.

History: no sign of moderation

After independence in 1838, Nicaragua was marked by a violent struggle for power between the Liberals, based in Leon, and the Conservatives, based in Granada. From 1855 to 1857 Nicaragua was ruled by an American buccaneer, William Walker, who had been invited in with a band of mercenaries by the Liberals and who proclaimed himself president. He was driven from office. After an American-backed coup in 1909, Nicaragua allowed the United States to run its customs and excise (raising money to pay the foreign debt), the national bank and the railway. When the marines left in 1933, they had been in Nicaragua for three decades. American dominance was replaced by the Somozas. In 1934 Anastasio Somoza, commander of the National Guard, had the rebel leader, Cesar Augusto Sandino, murdered although he had laid down his arms. Somoza and his sons Luis and Anastasio Jr ruled Nicaragua until 1979. They owned the main port, the main brewery, huge ranches, the biggest hotel, a cement company, the national airline and many other chunks of the economy.

The Sandinists take over

The Somozas were overthrown in 1979 by the Sandinist rebels. As their Marxist sympathies and anti-American rhetoric grew in intensity, the Sandinists lost their non-communist friends. Their party became identified with the state. Their secret police and their political prisons were much feared. Land was seized. Private businesses were nationalised. Ties with Cuba and the Soviet Union grew. The only opposition newspaper, *La Prensa*, was censored. The leader of the nine ruling *comandantes*, Daniel Ortega, was elected president in 1984; but the opposition candidate had withdrawn, saying there was no chance of the poll being free.

The contras respond

Men of the hated former National Guard formed a rebel force, financed by the United States, which became known as the contras. They harassed the Sandinists. Central American presidents and others sought to work out peaceful solutions. Eventually a settlement was reached: the United States would disarm the contras in return for iron-clad Sandinist guarantees that the presidential election in 1990 would be free. Never dreaming he might lose, President Ortega agreed. But the opposition candidate, Violeta Chamorro, publisher of *La Prensa*, swept the board.

Politics: the difficulties of cohabitation

In the period before Mrs Chamorro took office, the outgoing Sandinists made a grab for state and private property. Seeking national conciliation, Mrs Chamorro decided to "cohabit" with the Sandinists. Thus General Humberto Ortega, Daniel's brother, stayed on as army commander and Sandinists kept top jobs in the police and interior ministry. Mrs Chamorro's supporters, from businessmen to unionists, were appalled. So was the United States, which suspended its aid programme. All blamed Mrs Chamorro's influential son-in-law, Antonio Lacayo. But she persevered against the odds. Daniel Ortega boasted he was "governing from below" through Sandinist-led and strike-happy trade unions. In 1993 Mrs Chamorro announced that General Ortega would have to step down the following year. Although the army had been reduced, from 90,000 to 16,000 servicemen, and most of the contras had given up their weapons, many on both sides were still ready to resume the fight; several contra commanders had been murdered. Nonetheless Mrs Chamorro's policy had brought the country a badly needed period of peace and liberty.

The economy: low inflation

After bouts of hyper-inflation under the Sandinists (33,000% in 1988), the rate fell to 28.3% in 1993. Many state-owned enterprises have been privatised. But investors lack confidence in property laws. GDP fell by 1% in 1993 after growing by 0.8% in 1992 and falling slightly in each of the previous three years and hugely (13.6%) in calamitous 1988. Nicaragua's foreign trade is usually in deficit, depressed by low world prices for three principal exports: coffee, cotton and sugar. Lacking foreign investments, Nicaragua covers its trade deficit with income from foreign aid. Until it can create a stable business climate, the best that Nicaragua can hope is for the economy to stagnate.

Total area	129,494 sq km	% agricultural area	53
Capital	Managua	Highest point metres	Pico Mogotan 2,107
Other cities	Leon	Main rivers	Escondido, Grande de Malagalpa

The economy

GDP $bn	1.3	GDP per head $	410
% av. ann. growth in real GDP 1987–92	-2.7	GDP per head in purchasing power parity (USA=100)	11.5

Origins of GDP	*% of total*	**Components of GDP**	*% of total*
Agriculture	30	Private consumption	89
Industry	23	Public consumption	21
of which:		Investment	21
manufacturing	19	Exports	22
Services	47	Imports	-48

Structure of manufacturing

% of total

Agric. & food processing	...	Other	...
Textiles & clothing	...	Av. ann. increase in industrial output 1987–92	...
Machinery & transport	...		

Inflation and exchange rates

Consumer price 1993 av. ann. incr.	413.5%	Cordobas per $ av. 1993	...
Av. ann. rate 1987–93	...	Cordobas per ecu av. 1993	...

Balance of payments, reserves, aid and debt

$bn

Visible exports fob	0.2	Capital balance	-0.1
Visible imports fob	-0.7	Overall balance	-0.8
Trade balance	-0.5	Change in reserves	-0.02
Invisible inflows	0.1	Level of reserves end Dec.	...
Invisible outflows	-0.7	Foreign debt	11.1
Net transfers	0.4	as % of GDP	822.6
Current account balance	-0.7	Debt service	
as % of GDP	55.0[a]	as % of export earnings	26.5

Principal exports	*$m fob*	**Principal imports**	*$m cif*
Coffee	43	Raw materials & intermediate products	336
Meat	29	Consumer goods	270
Cotton	26	Capital goods	194
Sugar	22	Fuels & lubricants	109

Main export destinations	*% of total*	**Main origins of imports**	*% of total*
USA	16.4	USA	21.3
Germany	14.4	Cuba	8.0
Japan	11.0	Costa Rica	7.8
Canada	11.0	Venezuela	7.1

Government

System Republic. President is directly elected for a 6-year term. Unicameral National Assembly comprises 92 members directly elected by proportional representation.
Main political parties National Opposition Union (coalition of 14 parties), Sandinist National Liberation Front

Climate and topography

Tropical in lowlands, cooler in highlands. Extensive Atlantic coastal plains rising to central interior mountains. Narrow Pacific coastal plain interrupted by volcanoes.

People and society

Population m	4.1	% under 15	45.9
Pop. per sq km	32	% over 65	2.6
% urban	60	No. men per 100 women	101
% av. ann. growth 1987–92	3.4	Human Development Index	50.0
No. households m	...		

Life expectancy	*yrs*	**Education**	
Men	60	Spending as % of GDP	2.5
Women	66	Years of compulsory education	...
Crude birth rate	37	Adult literacy %	88
Crude death rate	7	Primary school enrolment %	75
Infant mortality		Secondary school enrolment %	38
per 1,000 live births	57	Tertiary education enrolment %	8

Workforce	*% of total*	**Consumer goods ownership**	
			Pop. per
Services	38		
Industry	16	Car	71.4
Agriculture	46	TV	16.1
% unemployed	...	Telephone	...

Ethnic groups	*% of total*	**Religious groups**	*% of total*
Mestizo	69	Roman Catholic	95
White	17	Protestant	5
Black	9		
Indian	5		

Tourism		**Health**	
Tourist arrivals m	0.1	Pop. per doctor	1,560
Tourist receipts $m	12		

a Estimate.

PANAMA

Total area	77,200 sq km	Population	2.5m
GDP	$6.1bn	GDP per head	$2,440
Capital	Panama City	Other cities	Colon, David

Panama is a country in search of an identity. It has been misruled and corrupted for decades by military rulers. Since General Manuel Antonio Noriega was ousted as the country's strongman by an American invasion ordered by President Bush in 1989, however, Panama has been ruled by civilians. They have revived the economy, established an open government and respected civil rights. But they have not impressed the voters.

History: an odd sort of independence

Independence from Spanish rule came in 1821. The Panamanians chose not to join the union of Central American provinces and turned eastward to become part of Gran Colombia, several hundred miles away through jungle. In 1903 the United States obtained, in a treaty with Colombia, the right to build a canal across the isthmus. After Colombian politicians protested, the United States encouraged Panamanians to rebel and seize independence. The new rulers signed a treaty with the United States which allowed it to build and operate the canal independently, thereby splitting the country in two.

The Arias difficulty

Panama was mostly ruled by presidents representing the landowners, traders and building companies. But not Arnulfo Arias, an unpredictable populist orator much loved by the crowds. In 1941 Arias was ousted from the presidency in a coup. He was subsequently robbed of the 1948 election by vote-rigging. He took office in 1949 after a coup but was impeached and banned from public life a year later. He bounced back in 1968, when he was elected president and ousted after 11 days in office, and in 1984, when he was again the victim of vote-rigging. The most powerful figure of the times was Colonel Omar Torrijos, who took power in 1968 and kept it until his death in a plane crash in 1981. Torrijos's main achievement was to sign in 1977, with President Jimmy Carter, a treaty under which America was to hand over the canal to Panama and withdraw troops by the end of 1999. (As this date came closer, Panama became edgier; there were voices expressing the hope that some American forces would remain.)

Politics: the Noriega nightmare

In 1982 General Manuel Antonio Noriega became commander of the National Guard and de facto ruler of Panama behind a democratic veneer. Noriega was corrupted by power. He helped drug-traffickers in Colombia and elsewhere, rigged elections, did deals with Cuba's President Castro and the American Central Intelligence Agency, and enriched himself. In 1989, as the candidate of an opposition alliance was heading for victory in a presidential election, General Noriega suspended the counting and was declared head of government. He was subsequently ousted in a controversial operation by American Marines ordered in by President Bush in December 1989, tried in an American court and jailed for 40 years on drugs charges. He was succeeded by Guillermo Endara, the frustrated victor in the presidential election. Mr Endara was a convinced democrat but an unconvincing president. And Panamanian society was in danger of being corrupted by drug-trafficking and money-laundering. Panamanians appeared to have lost faith in their democratic rulers. In May 1994 Ernesto Perez Balladares of the Democratic Revolutionary Party easily won the presidential election with a promise to root out corruption and reduce unemployment. But Mr Perez, nicknamed "The Bull" for his large frame and loud voice, was an associate of General Noriega and Torrijos.

Society: mixed and divided

Panama is a multi-ethnic society dominated by people of Spanish origin. A sizeable part of Panama City, on the Pacific coast, looks prosperous. But there are pockets of poverty. In the Caribbean port of Colon, where most of the people are black, unemployment is widespread and the region is a social tinderbox. President Endara was aware of the problem – but did little about it – despite riots in 1992. There is a small, protected Indian population.

The economy: rescued

Panama's economy is dominated by services: banking, insurance and arrangements to register a company to carry out foreign operations so that it does not have pay taxes in its home country. Under General Noriega its banks laundered millions of dollars in drug money (an operation that is said to have stopped when he was ousted). Under his discredited regime the GDP fell by 15.9% in 1988. It revived under sound management by Mr Endara's team. The GDP grew by 5.2% in 1990, 9.1% in 1991, 8% in 1992 and 5.5% in 1993. The fiscal deficit was cut. A free zone adjacent to Colon boomed.

Total area	78,200 sq km	% agricultural area	23
Capital	Panama City	Highest point metres	Volcan Bani 3,475
Other cities	Colon, David	Main rivers	Chagres

The economy

GDP $bn	6.1	GDP per head $	2,440
% av. ann. growth in real GDP 1987–92	0.9	GDP per head in purchasing power parity (USA=100)	22.2

Origins of GDP	*% of total*	**Components of GDP**	*% of total*
Agriculture	10	Private consumption	72
Industry	11	Public consumption	21
of which:		Investment	15
manufacturing	...	Exports	29
Services	79	Imports	-39

Structure of manufacturing

			% of total
Agric. & food processing	52	Other	39
Textiles & clothing	6	Av. ann. increase in industrial output 1987–92	...
Machinery & transport	3		

Inflation and exchange rates

Consumer price 1992 av. ann. incr.	1.8%	Balboas per $ av. 1993	1.00
Av. ann. rate 1987–92	0.9%	Balboas per ecu av. 1993	1.12

Balance of payments, reserves, aid and debt

			$bn
Visible exports fob	5.0	Capital balance	-0.8
Visible imports fob	-5.9	Overall balance	-0.5
Trade balance	-0.9	Change in reserves	-0.01
Invisible inflows	2.2	Level of reserves end Dec.	0.5
Invisible outflows	-1.6	Foreign debt	6.5
Net transfers	0.1	as % of GDP	111.8
Current account balance	-0.1	Debt service	
as % of GDP	-0.7	as % of export earnings	31.3

Principal exports[a]	*$m fob*	**Principal imports**[a]	*$m cif*
Bananas	191	Machinery & transport equip.	435
Shrimp and lobster	95	Mineral products	258
Sugar	24	Chemicals	204

Main export destinations	*% of total*	**Main origins of imports**	*% of total*
USA	31.9	USA	37.0
Germany	26.7	Japan	8.2
Italy	8.1	Ecuador	6.0
Costa Rica	6.6	Netherlands Antilles	3.1

Government

System Republic. President and 2 vice-presidents directly elected. Unicameral Legislative Assembly elected on a party basis.
Main political parties Democratic Revolutionary Party, Arnulfista Party, Christian Democratic Party

Climate and topography

Tropical; hot and humid, with prolonged rainy season from May to January. Rugged interior with steep mountains. Coastal areas largely plains and rolling hills.

People and society

Population m	2.5	% under 15	34.9
Pop. per sq km	32	% over 65	4.7
% urban	53	No. men per 100 women	104
% av. ann. growth 1987–92	2.0	Human Development Index	73.8
No. households m	...		

Life expectancy	*yrs*	**Education**	
Men	73	Spending as % of GDP	5.7
Women	77	Years of compulsory education	8
Crude birth rate	25	Adult literacy %	88
Crude death rate	5	Primary school enrolment %	92
Infant mortality		Secondary school enrolment %	59
per 1,000 live births	17	Tertiary education enrolment %	22

Workforce	*% of total*	**Consumer goods ownership**	
			Pop. per
Services	67		
Industry	21	Car	15.4
Agriculture	12	TV	6.1
% unemployed	13.6	Telephone	9.6

Ethnic groups	*% of total*	**Religious groups**	*% of total*
Mestizo	70	Roman Catholic	93
West Indian	14	Protestant	6
White	10		
Indian	6		

Tourism		**Health**	
Tourist arrivals m	0.2	Pop. per doctor	1,000
Tourist receipts $bn	0.2		

a 1991.

Part III

CARIBBEAN COUNTRY PROFILES

62 Anguilla
64 Antigua
66 The Bahamas
68 Barbados
70 Bermuda
72 Cayman Islands
74 Cuba
80 Dominica
82 Dominican Republic
86 Grenada
88 Guadeloupe
90 Haiti
94 Jamaica
98 Martinique
100 Montserrat
102 Netherlands Antilles and Aruba
104 Puerto Rico
108 St Kitts and Nevis
110 St Lucia
112 St Vincent and the Grenadines
114 Trinidad & Tobago
118 Turks and Caicos Islands
120 Virgin Islands (UK)
122 Virgin Islands (US)

ANGUILLA

Anguilla is a small British Caribbean colony with a population of less than 10,000 which enjoyed a moment of fame and has since lived quietly in the shadow of danger.

History: a Caribbean roar

In 1967 Anguilla was given "associate" status on the way to full independence but tied to two other islands, St Kitts and Nevis, and feared it would be dominated by them. Ronald Webster, leader of the People's Progressive Party, rejected the scheme. Negotiations failed and in 1969 British forces occupied the island. It became a British Dependent Territory, free from dreaded St Kitts. Anguilla achieved a brief moment of international fame as "the mouse that roared".

Politics: quiet on the surface

Under a British governor, Anguilla has since been run by a chief minister. Mr Webster was replaced in 1977 by Sir Emile Gumbs but bounced back to power in 1980 and lost again to Sir Emile in 1984. Relations between Sir Emile and British governors have been edgy.

The shadow over Anguilla is cast by the Dutch island of St Maarten, only 20 minutes away by boat, which has been a home to the Mafia and drug-traffickers. It is seen in Anguilla as a threat to law and order. Anguilla has been used for drug drops and traffickers have been buying up land. They could buy up the island if they felt so inclined. So far, however, Anguilla has escaped this fate. It has succeeded in remaining relatively unspoilt.

The economy: modesty prevails

The island has a small unemployment problem (6% in 1992) caused mainly by people with no training or qualifications. Skilled workers are in short supply and several hundreds have been admitted as immigrants. The islanders live off tourism and lobsters; they raise some cattle, repair boats and grow lettuce, yams, pigeon-peas and sweet potatoes for the hotel trade. Both stopover and day-tripper arrivals are increasing steadily. There is also an effort to attract offshore financial services to register themselves in Anguilla. The island runs a budget deficit, has to borrow locally and also relies heavily on outside assistance. But inflation is low (about 2% in 1992). Anguilla is trying to be self-sufficient. The European Union has provided a grant to improve the inadequate water supply and roads.

Total area	91 sq km	% agricultural area	...
Capital	The Valley	Highest point metres	Crocus Hill 65

The economy

GDP $m	56.8	GDP per head $	5,652
% av. ann. growth in real GDP 1985–92	...	GDP per head in purchasing power parity (USA=100)	...

Origins of GDP	*% of total*	**Components of GDP**	*% of total*
Agriculture	4	Private consumption	...
Industry	4	Public consumption	...
of which:		Investment	...
manufacturing	1	Exports	...
Services	94	Imports	...

Government

System British dependent territory with governor. House of Assembly consists of a Speaker, Deputy Speaker, 7 elected members, 2 nominated members, and 2 ex-officio members.

Main political parties Anguilla National Alliance, Anguilla United Party, Anguilla Democratic Party

Climate and topography

Most northerly of Leeward Islands, 270 km east of Puerto Rico. Consists of island of Sombrero and several other offshore islets. Low rainfall. Flat low-lying terrain of coral and limestone.

People and society

Population	9,700	% under 15	...
Pop. per sq km	76	% over 65	...
% urban	...	No. men per 100 women	...
% av. ann. growth 1987–92	nil	No. households m	...
Human Development Index	...		

Ethnic groups	*% of total*	**Religious groups**	*% of total*
Mainly Black African		Anglican	40
		Methodist	33
		Seventh-Day Adventist	7
		Baptist	5
		Roman Catholic	3
		Other	12

ANTIGUA

Independent from Britain since 1967 as a member of the Commonwealth with Queen Elizabeth as head of state, Antigua has been ruled by one of the patriarchs of the English-speaking Caribbean, Vere Bird Sr, from 1946 to 1971 and from 1976 to 1994 when he resigned in favour of one of his sons, Lester. Such a long period in power produced the inevitable result: the image of an island oligarchy. Antigua has been described by a well-placed diplomat as "an embarrassment to Britain".

Politics: a fall from grace

Mr Bird and his sons, Vere Jr and Lester, at the top of the Labour Party, have exercised much power. Vere Bird Jr fell from grace after it was discovered in 1991 that, as minister in charge of national security, he had links to a shipment of arms from Israel, sent to a fictitious address in Antigua. The shipment was sent on to Panama and ended up in the hands of a Colombian drug baron. There was talk of a military training school being set up in Antigua. A report on the affair by a senior British barrister was highly critical of some government ministers. Vere Bird Jr remained in parliament. Other ministers were accused of corruption including the finance minister, Molwyn Joseph, who was alleged in 1992 to have taken bribes from a construction company. Several banks were under investigation. In 1994 the ruling party went into a general election holding 15 of the 17 parliamentary seats. (The others were held by the opposition United Progressive Party, which had the support of the chamber of commerce and the small-business association, and a representative from Barbuda.) It lost four seats.

The economy: a house in disorder

The main job-provider is tourism, accounting for 60% of GDP. Cotton and fishing have been expanding but an oil refinery and a sugar factory were closed. The fiscal deficit has been covered through the accumulation of arrears to domestic and foreign creditors. In 1992 outstanding external debt amounted to 80% of GDP. To put things right, the government needed to cut spending, increase revenues and sell off state-owned hotels. While the Bird government stayed in office, the prospects of that happening, and of Antigua attracting legitimate, job-creating investments appeared dim. The Caribbean Development Bank said the government should "act swiftly to restore the country's credit-worthiness as well as improve its fiscal performance".

Total area	440 sq km	% agricultural area	25
Capital	Saint John's	Highest point metres	Boggy Peak 405
Other cities	Codrington		

The economy

GDP $m	395	GDP per head $	4,870
% av. ann. growth in real GDP 1987–92	4.7	GDP per head in purchasing power parity (USA=100)	...

Government

System Constitutional monarchy and parliamentary democracy with governor-general representing Queen Elizabeth II. Bicameral legislature.
Main political parties Antigua Labour Party, United Progressive Party

Climate and topography

Tropical climate, but milder than most West Indian islands. Hot season from May to November. Mean rainfall 40 inches. Mostly low-lying limestone and coral islands with some higher volcanic areas. Lies 420 km east-southeast of Puerto Rico.

People and society

Population	70,000	% under 15	38.0
Pop. per sq km	159	% over 65	5.1
% urban	31	No. men per 100 women	93
% av. ann. growth 1987–92	3.1	No. households m	...
Human Development Index	78.5		

Ethnic groups	*% of total*	**Religious groups**	*% of total*
Mainly Black African		Anglican	90

THE BAHAMAS

The Bahamas have a warm climate, beautiful beaches, a friendly people and proximity to their most important market: the United States. They are also on a route for the smuggling of drugs from Colombia to North America.

History: the "Bay Street Boys"

The Bahamas were controlled for many years by a white elite based on Bay Street, the main commercial thoroughfare of Nassau. But the influence of the Bay Street Boys faded after independence in 1967 when a predominantly black party, led by Lynden Pindling, won a general election.

Politics: the old order passes

After 25 years in power, Sir Lynden Pindling (as he later became) and his Progressive Liberal Party were unseated in a general election in August 1992. The campaign focused on allegations of corruption and economic mismanagement. The conservative Free National Movement won 31 seats against 17 for the ruling party. Its leader, Hubert Ingraham, became prime minister. It was the end of an era during which the United States was concerned about drug-trafficking: Carlos Lehder, a Colombian drug baron subsequently jailed in the United States, owned a small island and used its airstrip for drug flights. Damning testimony might have been given in an American court incriminating a senior Bahamian. No trial took place. This non-event was followed in the 1980s by a period of close co-operation on drugs between the government and the United States.

The economy: beaches and banks

Tourism provides over half of GDP and 70% of the islands' jobs. The 700-odd islands and 2,000 uninhabited cays are ideal for visitors and attracted the New World's first tourist, Christopher Columbus, who landed at San Salvador, or Watling Island, in 1492. The Bahamas are also an offshore banking centre. At the end of 1992 more than 10,000 international companies were registered there. There is also a free-trade zone at Freeport. Mr Ingraham planned to privatise and to encourage foreign investment to improve the government's shaky finances. The overall budget deficit fell under his government but was still too high, as was the foreign debt at $485m in 1992. The government should reduce its dependence on tourism by investing more in agriculture and fishing.

Total area	13,940 sq km	% agricultural area	nil
Capital	Nassau	Highest point metres	Mount Alvernia 63

The economy

GDP $bn	3.2	GDP per head $	12,020
% av. ann. growth in real GDP 1987–92	1.3	GDP per head in purchasing power parity (USA=100)	...

Origins of GDP	*% of total*	**Components of GDP**	*% of total*
Agriculture	5	Private consumption	64
Industry	39	Public consumption	12
of which:		Investment	19
manufacturing	10	Exports	61
Services	56	Imports	-56

Government

System Constitutional monarchy and parliamentary democracy with governor-general representing Queen Elizabeth II. Bicameral legislature.
Main political parties Progressive Liberal Party, Free National Movement

Climate and topography

Tropical marine climate moderated by Gulf Stream. Long flat coral formations with some low rounded hills.

People and society

Population	259,000	% under 15	31.8
Pop. per sq km	19	% over 65	4.3
% urban	...	No. men per 100 women	99
% av. ann. growth 1987–92	1.6	No. households m	...
Human Development Index	87.5		

Ethnic groups	*% of total*	**Religious groups**	*% of total*
Black	85	Baptist	32
White	15	Anglican	20
		Roman Catholic	19
		Methodist	6

BARBADOS

Barbados has been living beyond its means. This charming island, stable and serene with its manicured golf courses and gorgeous views of the Caribbean, is over-paid, over-indebted, inefficient and running into trouble.

Politics: a question of colour

Independence came in 1966 after the collapse of the West Indies Federation (led by a distinguished Barbadian, Sir Grantley Adams). Since then the island has had a two-party system pitting the black-nationalist Democratic Labour Party against the Barbados Labour Party, which was accused of being financed by, and favouring, the lighter-coloured elite. In the 1990s there have been some dodgy land deals and unexplained resignations. A health minister has been censured for irregularities in public accounts.

The economy: too many misjudgments

Barbadian governments created an over-large state sector and borrowed too much to pay their debts. Wages have risen too fast; investors looking for cheap labour tried Barbados and turned to cheaper spots. A big trade deficit led to a crisis in 1991 when the government had to defend the currency with an interest rate of 18%.

Bitter-sweet

Barbados's sugar industry has four mills but needs two. The British firm Booker has been invited to help. Fortunately Barbadian farmers have diversified into new crops and done well. For years Barbados catered mainly for wealthy holidaymakers. In the early 1990s it went downmarket, to no great effect. A warning from the American State Department about increased crime in Barbados did not help.

The hesitator could lose

The prime minister, Erskine Sandiford, who took over in 1987, said he favoured privatising a dairy, a flour mill and the bus service but displayed little enthusiasm. He did, however, announce in 1992 a tax reform. The basic rate went from 20% to 25% and the top rate was cut by 10% to 40%. Tax relief was abolished for mortgage interest, life insurance and pension contributions. The economy appeared to have stabilised by the end of 1992. But the Caribbean Development Bank said: "The government must act to increase investment; expand the export sector; make labour more mobile; liberalise trade and generally restore international competitiveness."

Total area	430 sq km	% agricultural area	77
Capital	Bridgetown	Highest point metres	Mount Hillaby 340

The economy

GDP $bn	1.7	GDP per head $	6,530
% av. ann. growth in real GDP 1987–92	-1.0	GDP per head in purchasing power parity (USA=100)	...

Origins of GDP	*% of total*	**Components of GDP**	*% of total*
Agriculture	5	Private consumption	67
Industry	28	Public consumption	19
of which:		Investment	17
manufacturing	6	Exports	45
Services	67	Imports	48

Principal exports	*$m fob*	**Principal imports**	*$m cif*
Sugar & molasses	32	Machinery	138
Chemicals	22	Food & beverages	99
Electrical components	21	Construction materials	29

Government

System Constitutional monarchy and parliamentary democracy with governor-general representing Queen Elizabeth II. Bicameral legislature.
Main political parties Democratic Labor Party, Barbados Labor Party, National Democratic Party (split from DLP in 1989)

Climate and topography

Tropical with rainy season from June to October. Relatively flat terrain rising gently to central highland region.

People and society

Population	260,000	% under 15	24.5
Pop. per sq km	605	% over 65	11.3
% urban	45	No. men per 100 women	93
% av. ann. growth 1987–92	0.8	No. households m	...
Human Development Index	92.8		

Ethnic groups	*% of total*	**Religious groups**	*% of total*
African	80	Anglican	40
Mixed	16	Pentecostal	8
European	4	Methodist	7
		Roman Catholic	4

BERMUDA

Out on its own in the Atlantic, Bermuda's fate is tied to the tourist trade. The statistics that matter are the visitors who fly in for a weekend or a week or two, and those who stop at the island aboard a cruise liner. The statistics have not been promising. Bermudans are finding that, despite their island's natural attractions, the tourism market is fiercely competitive.

History: a stable course

Bermuda is a British crown colony, with a governor and a premier, Sir John Swan, leader of the moderate, multi-racial United Bermuda Party (of the island's population of 60,000, some 35,600 are black). Bermuda boasts that it is the oldest self-governing British colony and that its parliament is the third oldest in the world (it opened in 1620). Its history has been uneventful. Sir John, who took office 1982, has 22 seats in the House of Assembly; the opposition Labour Party has 18. In 1994 Sir John was promoting the idea of independence. This would probably be decided after a referendum. The United States and Britain said they would close their military bases to cut costs. (This would prove to be expensive since the Americans have run the island's airport.)

Murder of the governor

The most dramatic event in recent history occurred in 1976 when two men were executed for the murders of the governor, Sir Richard Sharples, his aide-de-camp, the police commissioner and two businessmen. After the executions, riots and arson erupted in Hamilton and elsewhere. They were put down by the British army.

The economy: the downturn

Tourism accounts for roughly 36% of GDP and 60% of export earnings, followed by offshore financial services (especially the booming re-insurance business) with 22% of GDP and 40% of exports. But the number of tourists visiting Bermuda has in recent years been falling because of the downturn in the American economy (most of the tourists come from the United States), and the over-selling of the island. There are too many tourists on mopeds for such a small place and Bermuda has been over-priced – although it has for years succeeded in attracting upmarket visitors. The decline has helped to keep inflation below American levels. This should help to restore competitiveness. Bermudans hoped tourism would revive as the American recession ended.

Total area	50 sq km	% agricultural area	nil
Capital	Hamilton	Highest point metres	Town Hill 79

The economy

GDP $m[a]	1.4	GDP per head $	...
% av. ann. growth in real GDP 1987–92	...	GDP per head in purchasing power parity (USA=100)	...

Government

System British dependent territory, with representative government. Governor is appointed by UK monarch with special responsibilities for defence and external affairs. Bicameral parliament.
Main political parties United Bermuda Party, Progressive Labour Party, National Liberal Party

Climate and topography

Subtropical, mild and humid. Strong winds common in winter. Comprises 150 small islands (about 20 inhabited) in western Atlantic, 1,050 km east of North Carolina in USA.

People and society

Population	60,000	% under 15	...
Pop. per sq km	1,200	% over 65	...
% urban	...	No. men per 100 women	...
% av. ann. growth 1987–92	nil	No. households m	...
Human Development Index	...		

Ethnic groups	*% of total*	**Religious groups**	*% of total*
Black	61	Anglican	37
White	39	Roman Catholic	14
		African Methodist Episcopal	10
		Methodist	6
		Seventh-Day Adventist	5

a 1990.

CAYMAN ISLANDS

The three Cayman Islands, first sighted by Christopher Columbus in 1503, were for decades a hideout for pirates and other villains. The only industry now is tourism. The principal business is that of being a tax haven. At times the islands have also served as stopover points for drug-traffickers.

History: a tie to Jamaica

The main island, Grand Cayman, was taken over as a colony in 1670. All three were administered from Jamaica until Jamaican independence, when they were run from George Town by a British governor, an executive council and an assembly.

The economy: a super-haven

Following the introduction of secrecy laws for its bank accounts in the late 1960s, the islands became an offshore financial centre. One of the banks attracted was the Bank of Credit and Commerce International (BCCI). There were 25,000 companies registered at the end of 1992 compared with 23,700 at the end of 1991. There were more than 500 offshore banks and some 365 insurance companies. There is no income or corporate tax. The fact that BCCI made use of the Cayman Islands' facilities in its criminal schemes raised questions about offshore banking. But it was concluded that if the Caymans did not do it, others would (and already did). In the early 1990s an attempt was being made to clean up the system and the American government was given access to bank accounts if investigators could prove that the account was being used for criminal purposes.

Tourists matter too

About a quarter of the 9,000-strong workforce is employed in tourism. There is some fishing, but catching turtles for export virtually stopped after the United States banned imports. The economy is strong: GDP in 1992 grew by 4% after an extraordinary 13.2% in 1990. The budget deficit has been rising, however, partly because of an ambitious public-works programme. The government was trying to raise more taxes and trim expenses through privatisation. One of the difficulties is a shortage of skilled labour. To remedy this, the government has been planning to build a community college. Tourism was expected to pick up as the American economy improved and the economy was expected to remain fairly strong.

Total area	260 sq km	% agricultural area	8
Capital	George Town	Highest point metres	Cayman Brac 42

The economy

GDP $m	570.7	GDP per head $	18,137
% av. ann. growth in real GDP 1985–92	...	GDP per head in purchasing power parity (USA=100)	...

Origins of GDP	*% of total*	**Components of GDP**	*% of total*
Agriculture	0	Private consumption	...
Industry	3	Public consumption	...
of which:		Investment	...
manufacturing	2	Exports	...
Services	97	Imports	...

Government

System British dependent territory with governor appointed by the Crown. Unicameral legislative assembly.

Main political parties No formal parties

Climate and topography

Tropical marine with warm, rainy summers and cool, relatively dry winters. Three islands located about 520 km west of Jamaica. Low-lying limestone base surrounded by coral reefs.

People and society

Population	29,140	% under 15	...
Pop. per sq km	112	% over 65	...
% urban	...	No. men per 100 women	...
% av. ann. growth 1987–92	nil	No. households m	...
Human Development Index	...		

Ethnic groups	*% of total*	**Religious groups**	*% of total*
Mixed	40	Protestant	98
White	20		
Black	20		

CUBA

Total area	110,860 sq km	Population	10.8m
GDP	$20.3bn	GDP per head	$1,880
Capital	Havana	Other cities	Santiago, Camaguey

With the collapse of communism in the former Soviet Union and Eastern Europe, the days of the government of President Fidel Castro in Cuba appeared in 1994 to be numbered. However, its inevitable collapse seemed unlikely to erase the mark which the Cuban revolution under Mr Castro had left, for better and for worse, on the western hemisphere and the world.

History: an island of strongmen

Under Spanish colonial rule, Cuba became a sugar monoculture. About 90% of its exports went to the United States. A rebellion (1868–78) ended with the insurgents surrendering in return for freedom for rebel slaves and the extension of political rights. In the following years slavery was abolished. Observing Cuba's steady absorption into the United States, Spain abrogated its trade agreement with the latter and precipitated a bigger rebellion in which a prominent nationalist, Jose Marti, who was to become Cuba's national hero, died.

American intervention

The Americans sent the *USS Maine* to Havana harbour in 1898, where it blew up with the loss of 266 American lives. This was taken as a *casus belli*: American forces invaded and took the island. The United States governed Cuba for four years, and improved the education and public-health services. It gave Cuba its independence in 1902 but retained the right to intervene under the so-called Platt Amendment. Until 1933 Cuba was ruled by an assortment of generals ending with Carlos Machado (1925–33). It was a period marked by unrest, especially among Havana University students. Eventually, after a sergeants' revolt, Fulgencio Batista became the dominant figure; in 1934 he crushed the student movement and ruled from 1934 to 1959 through an alliance with the Cuban Communist Party and the army.

Enter Castro

One of the student leaders was Fidel Castro, the son of a prosperous Spanish immigrant. In 1953 he led an unsuccessful attack on the Moncada barracks at Santiago and was jailed, in comfort, for 11 months. In 1956 he sailed with a small group to Cuba from Mexico aboard a yacht, the *Granma*, and landed at Los Cayuelos. But he suffered reverses and took refuge in the Sierra Maestra mountains with 12 followers. Using the mountains as a base, Castro launched attacks and his brother, Raul, kidnapped foreign businessmen. Batista's repression and corruption grew increasingly unpopular. The United States suspended its supply of arms to him. With an increasing band of supporters, Castro began an advance from the mountains on Havana. Support for Batista dissolved and he fled to Miami. Castro entered Havana a national hero in 1959.

Politics: the "maximum leader"

Mr Castro became prime minister and began a reign of terror. Numerous men associated with the Batista regime were taken away and shot, some of them after summary televised trials. Others were jailed for long terms for what were political crimes. Virtually the entire middle class emigrated to Miami. Like Batista, Castro formed an alliance with the Communist Party. His communist contact was Carlos Rafael Rodriguez, who had served Batista as labour minister. Mr Rodriguez became a key figure in the Castro regime. The entire private sector, with the exception of smallholdings, was expropriated. Trade unions, independent media and opposition parties were closed down. Many Cuban nationalists who had fought alongside Castro or supported him in other ways abandoned his regime.

Hatred of America

Throughout, Mr Castro's actions were guided by a visceral anti-Americanism. His nationalisations of American property and his insults against *yanquis* and *gringos* and *imperialismo* were bound, he knew, to provoke the United States and they did. President Eisenhower broke relations and started a trade embargo. In 1961 President Kennedy authorised an invasion of the island by an exile army based in Guatemala but the landing area was a disastrous mistake, Kennedy withdrew air cover at the last minute and the operation at the Bay of Pigs failed. Mr Castro exulted in this triumph over imperialism. Later that year Mr Castro declared he was a Marxist-Leninist rather than a "humanitarian socialist". Instead of depending on the American market and the United States government for economic aid, Cuba turned to the Soviet Union. Its leader, Nikita Khrushchev, bought Cuba's sugar at subsidised prices and provided the Cuban leader with arms. Mr Castro began to finance and train guerrillas from other Latin American countries.

The Cuban missile crisis

In 1962 President Kennedy installed American Thor missiles in Turkey, a 15-minute flight from Moscow, and Khrushchev responded by assigning Soviet missiles to Cuba. This clandestine operation was spotted while the missiles were on the high seas. Kennedy imposed a quarantine on Cuba barring the Soviet freighters from reaching the island. An east-west nuclear confrontation traumatised the world for 13 days. It was settled by the withdrawal of the Soviet and American missiles and an American guarantee not to invade Cuba again. Mr Castro, who at one point wrote to Khrushchev urging him to bomb the United States, was kept out of the high-level bargaining and was furious.

Communist orthodoxy

Subsequently Mr Castro imposed orthodox communist forms of government on Cuba, becoming First Secretary of the Cuban Communist Party. This regime meant that while nobody was destitute and education and medical care were free, the economy decayed (theft of state property became widespread) and the political repression was stifling. The upshot was that, in a world of rigid state censorship, Cubans tended to believe what their "maximum leader", a charismatic orator, told them in his long and rambling speeches. Mr Castro also abolished the national holidays for Christmas and Easter.

Proletarian internationalism

In association with the Soviet Union, Cuba spread its influence in a remarkable way. Rebels in El Salvador, Guatemala and Nicaragua had the closest of contacts, including training, in Cuba. So did the small band of Marxist revolutionaries who seized power temporarily on the Caribbean island of Grenada. Thousands of Cuban soldiers and airmen were assigned to help the Marxist government of Angola to fight South African-backed rebels. Another big unit was sent to Ethiopia to help the Marxist regime there. Smaller groups of advisers went to other African countries. Mr Castro became a leading light of the Non-Aligned Movement regardless of his alignment to the Soviet Union. When proposals were made for investigations of his respect for human rights at the UN's Commission on Human Rights, third-world dictatorships plus the communist states invariably voted them down. It was only in 1989, when the United States was represented at the Commission by a naturalised Cuban who had spent 22 years as a political prisoner, and Eastern Europe was being transformed, that the vote went the other way.

The collapse of communism

Mr Castro showed no sign of being diverted from his course of anti-American, traditional communism when the regimes of Eastern Europe and the Soviet Union itself collapsed at the end of the 1980s and in the early 1990s. The only hint of change was a decision in November 1992 to allow independents to stand for election to the rubber-stamp parliament. At the same time, however, the practice of jailing or harassing dissidents continued. Most of this small and brave band were in jail in 1992 on charges of "enemy propaganda" or insulting communism. Mr Castro continued to blame the American trade "blockade" (actually an embargo) for Cuba's woes although Cuba could buy western goods from European countries and Latin America.

Society: not quite multi-racial

While most Cubans are of Spanish extraction there is a large black population. Cuban music and dancing reflects their African roots. The lot of blacks relative to whites has probably improved during the revolutionary years. But there are few blacks in the highest echelons of the Communist Party. How would Cuban society change after the fall of Castro? The experience of the Cuban emigrants who settled in Florida suggests that the people of the island are naturally adept at banking, commerce and industry.

The economy: a need for diversification

When Mr Castro came to power in 1959, Cuba's economy was dangerously dependent on sugar, rum and cigars. By the 1990s not much had changed. The main new products were zinc (Cuba possesses the fourth largest reserves in the world), citrus, textiles and consumer durables. No real attempt had been made to diversify. The attraction of selling sugar to the former Soviet block at highly subsidised prices was irresistible. Added to the deal was access to more Soviet oil than Cuba needed, at bargain prices. Cuba sold the excess for hard currency. All was well while the Soviet goose laid golden eggs. But the goose died. Thereafter, with no subsidies, no guaranteed market for its sugar, and no oil except at world market prices in hard currency, the Cuban economy went rapidly downhill. Reforms in 1993 permitting the free use of the dollar, letting individual Cubans work for themselves in certain businesses and encouraging joint enterprises, especially in tourism, had little effect.

Total area	110,860 sq km	% agricultural area	52
Capital	Havana	Highest point metres	Pico
Other cities	Santiago de Cuba, Camaguey, Holguin		Turquino 1,974

The economy

GDP $bn	20.3	GDP per head $	1,880
% av. ann. growth in real GDP 1987–92	...	GDP per head in purchasing power parity (USA=100)	...

Origins of GDP[a]	*% of total*	**Components of GDP**[b]	*% of total*
Agriculture	15	Private consumption	94
Industry	46	Public consumption	9
of which:		Investment	16
manufacturing	...	Exports	...
Services	39	Imports	...

Structure of manufacturing

% of total

Agric. & food processing	...	Other	...
Textiles & clothing	...	Av. ann. increase in industrial	
Machinery & transport	...	output 1987–92	...

Inflation and exchange rates

Consumer price 1993 av. ann. incr.	...	Pesos per $ av. 1993	0.76
Av. ann. rate 1987–93	...	Pesos per ecu av. 1993	...

Balance of payments, reserves, aid and debt

bn pesos

Visible exports fob	2.3	Capital balance	...
Visible imports fob	-2.5	Overall balance	...
Trade balance	-0.2	Change in reserves	...
Invisible inflows	...	Level of reserves end Dec.	...
Invisible outflows	...	Foreign debt	...
Net transfers	...	as % of GDP	...
Current account balance	...	Debt service	
as % of GDP	...	as % of export earnings	...

Principal exports	*bn pesos fob*	**Principal imports**	*bn pesos cif*
Sugar	1.2	Fuels & lubricants	1.2
Minerals	0.2	Machinery & transport equip.	0.8
Fruit & vegetables	0.2	Food & beverages	0.7
Fish products	0.1		

Main export destinations[c]	*% of total*	**Main origins of imports**[c]	*% of total*
Eastern Europe	81.9	Eastern Europe	84.9
Asia	7.3	EU	5.3
EU	7.1	Asia	3.9
Africa	1.2	Aladi	4.0

Government

System Communist republic with legislative power vested in the National Assembly of People's Power. Assembly elects a 31-member council of state as permanent organ. Fidel Castro has been president of council since 1976.

Main political parties Cuban Communist Party

Climate and topography

Tropical, moderated by trade winds; rainy season between May and October. Mostly flat to rolling plains, with rugged hills and mountains in southeast.

People and society

Population m	10.8	% under 15	22.8
Pop. per sq km	98	% over 65	8.4
% urban	75	No. men per 100 women	103
% av. ann. growth 1987–92	1.0	Human Development Index	71.1
No. households m	...		

Life expectancy	*yrs*	**Education**	
Men	74	Spending as % of GDP	6.7
Women	79	Years of compulsory education	8
Crude birth rate	17	Adult literacy %	94
Crude death rate	6	Primary school enrolment %	95
Infant mortality		Secondary school enrolment %	89
per 1,000 live births	11	Tertiary education enrolment %	21

Workforce	*% of total*	**Consumer goods ownership**	
			Pop. per
Services	47		
Industry	29	Car	45.5
Agriculture	24	TV	4.8
% unemployed	...	Telephone	19.2

Ethnic groups	*% of total*	**Religious groups**	*% of total*
Mulatto	51	Roman Catholic[d]	85
White	37		
Black	11		
Chinese	1		

Tourism[d]		**Health**	
Tourist arrivals m	0.4	Pop. per doctor	530
Tourist receipts $m	48		

a 1989.
b 1987.
c 1988.
d 1991.

DOMINICA

Dominica is a poor-but-honest English-speaking Caribbean island republic and former British colony. Before independence it was first part of the Leeward Islands then of the Windwards and became a separate entity in 1960. Independence came in 1978.

Politics: the story of one woman

Dame Eugenia Charles, elder stateswoman of the Caribbean, has governed the island since 1980 at the head of the Dominica Freedom Party. In 1981 she overcame an attempted coup by a former chief minister, Patrick John. The conservative and imposing Dame Eugenia sought American and British aid and, in return, was ready to co-operate out of conviction as well as national interest. When the United States and the Organisation of Eastern Caribbean States invaded Grenada to oust its Marxist junta in 1983, Miss Charles stood by President Reagan's side.

The economy: bananas...

The fate of Miss Charles's government, and of Dominica itself, has depended on the price obtained for the island's high-cost bananas, which provide about 40% of export revenue. Until the formation of the European Union's single market, Dominica and other islands of the former British West Indies enjoyed privileged access to the British banana market at a survivable price. Under the single market, however, lower-cost Latin American banana producers were pressing for greater access. An uneasy compromise was agreed with the help of Britain. But subsequently the deal was challenged and a long battle seemed inevitable. Although limited by the EU, large quantities of Latin American bananas appeared to be entering the market and depressing prices. This was undermining confidence. So was the low world price in the early 1990s of coconuts, Dominica's second most important export. Meanwhile farmers were turning to other money-earners: furniture, cut flowers, ginger, yams and plantains.

...and tourism

Total visitor arrivals increased from 45,500 in 1988 to 141,600 in 1992. Inflation is roughly 5% a year. GDP grew by 2.5% in 1992. The main cause for concern is the budget deficit and rising indebtedness. Dame Eugenia increased the consumption tax from 20% to 25% to cover the budget deficit in 1993.

Total area	750 sq km	% agricultural area	25
Capital	Roseau	Highest point metres	Morne Diablotin 1,447

The economy

GDP $m	181	GDP per head $	2,520
% av. ann. growth in real GDP 1987–92	3.6	GDP per head in purchasing power parity (USA=100)	...

Origins of GDP	*% of total*	**Components of GDP**	*% of total*
Agriculture	26	Private consumption	59
Industry	7	Public consumption	18
of which:		Investment	22
manufacturing	7	Exports	38
Services	67	Imports	-59

Principal exports	*$m fob*	**Principal imports**	*$m cif*
Bananas	31	...	
Toilet & laundry soap	12		

Government

System Republic and parliamentary democracy. Unicameral national assembly of 21 elected and 9 nominated members. Speaker is selected from either house or outside.

Main political parties Dominica Freedom Party, Dominica Labour Party, United Workers Party

Climate and topography

Tropical with heavy rainfall. Temperature is moderated by trade winds. Rugged mountains of volcanic origin.

People and society

Population	71,790	% under 15	37.5
Pop. per sq km	93	% over 65	8.3
% urban	41	No. men per 100 women	100
% av. ann. growth 1987–92	nil	No. households m	...
Human Development Index	81.9		

Ethnic groups	*% of total*	**Religious groups**	*% of total*
Black/Caribbean Indian	95	Roman Catholic	77
		Methodist	5
		Pentecostal	3
		Seventh-Day Adventist	3
		Baptist	2

DOMINICAN REP.

Total area	48,730 sq miles	Population	7.5m
GDP	$7.6bn	GDP per head	$1,040
Capital	Santo Domingo	Other cities	Santiago de los Caballeros

For much of this century, the Dominican Republic has been dominated by two leaders: Generalissimo Rafael Trujillo and Joaquin Balaguer, both in their different ways quintessential Latin American strongmen. This volatile, poor Caribbean country has suffered rebellion, invasion and occupation but has enjoyed an episode or two of democracy.

History: unsettled times

Christopher Columbus discovered the island which the Dominican Republic now shares with Haiti in 1492, when it was occupied by the Taino Indians. The Indians were enslaved and many died of diseases introduced from Spain. Needing workers on the sugar plantations that were established in the mid-16th century, the Spaniards imported African slaves. Independence of the Dominican Republic from Haiti came in 1844 after many disputes. In the 20th century the country has been unstable except during its occupation by American marines (1916–24), because the government could not pay its foreign debts, and during the dictatorship of Trujillo (1930–61), who ruled through murder, torture and blackmail but gained popularity with public-works programmes. When Trujillo was assassinated in a highway ambush in 1961, Mr Balaguer was the puppet president. He fled to New York.

Politics: call in the marines

A year later, a free election was won by Juan Bosch, an exiled social democrat whose mercurial temperament destroyed his chance of consolidating democracy. He was ousted in a coup after only seven months. There followed an unsuccessful interregnum and a rebellion led by young democratic army officers. Under pressure from President Lyndon Johnson the Organisation of American States sent a mostly American peace-keeping force of 23,000 men to restore order. Another election was held in 1966 and won by Mr Balaguer, back from exile and reminding voters of the Trujillo era of order and stability. Mr Balaguer won re-election twice (with some opposition parties boycotting the poll on the ground that it would be rigged) and ruled from 1966 to 1978. He was succeeded by two leaders of the opposition Dominican Revolutionary Party: Antonio Guzman (1978–82) and Salvador Jorge Blanco (1982–86). Neither was able to solve the country's economic difficulties and both suffered from party squabbles. So in 1986 Mr Balaguer bounced back again, and he was re-elected in 1990. His apparent narrow victory in 1994 was challenged by opposition parties which said the result was rigged.

Society: mixed and volatile

To celebrate the 500th anniversary of the arrival of Columbus, Mr Balaguer commissioned a giant lighthouse costing at least $70m that beams a cross on the sky above the capital. Pope John Paul declined an invitation to inaugurate it during a visit in 1992. The Dominican Republic is dominated by people of Spanish or mixed origin. Many of its poor are black. Widespread poverty and high unemployment have led many Dominicans to emigrate to the United States or to become drug-traffickers.

The economy: hopeful signs

In 1990 Mr Balaguer began a new presidential term in trouble: inflation was at 100% a year and there were severe shortages of fuel, food, water and electricity. He cut public spending by abolishing subsidies on food, energy, petrol and state enterprises, ran a tight-money policy and cut financing of state enterprises. The result was that inflation sank to 3% in 1993. GDP, which fell by 5% in 1990, rose by 7% in 1992 and 2% in 1993. By 1992 the country was on good terms with its international creditors.

Diversification pays

Once dependent on sugar, the Dominican economy has diversified. Now row after row of pineapples, mangoes, melons, vegetables, citrus trees and flowers-for-export grow where low-priced sugar-cane was once supreme. Nickel, mined by Falconbridge Dominicana, has overtaken sugar as the country's top foreign-exchange earner. Tourism, once geared to the American market, draws large numbers of Canadians and West Europeans as well to magnificent north-coast beaches. As a beneficiary of President Reagan's Caribbean Basin Initiative, the Dominican Republic enjoys low-tariff or no-tariff access to the United States for many exports. Nonetheless, the country has a long way to go: unemployment is put at 25% of the workforce and the principal problem is poverty.

Total area	48,730 sq km	% agricultural area	73
Capital	Santo Domingo	Highest point metres	Pico
Other cities	Santiago de los Caballeros, La Romana		Durate 3,175

The economy

GDP $bn	7.6	GDP per head $	1,040
% av. ann. growth in real GDP 1987–92	3.1	GDP per head in purchasing power parity (USA=100)	13.9

Origins of GDP	*% of total*	**Components of GDP**	*% of total*
Agriculture	18	Private consumption	77
Industry	25	Public consumption	9
of which:		Investment	17
manufacturing	13	Exports	27
Services	57	Imports	-41

Structure of manufacturing

			% of total
Agric. & food processing	...	Other	...
Textiles & clothing	...	Av. ann. increase in industrial output 1987–92	...
Machinery & transport	...		

Inflation and exchange rates

Consumer price 1992 av. ann. incr.	4.6%	Pesos per $ av. 1993	12.68
Av. ann. rate 1986–93	40.0%	Pesos per ecu av. 1993	14.20

Balance of payments, reserves, aid and debt

			$bn
Visible exports fob	0.6	Capital balance	0.04
Visible imports fob	-2.2	Overall balance	0.04
Trade balance	-1.6	Change in reserves	0.1
Invisible inflows	1.6	Level of reserves end Dec.	0.5
Invisible outflows	-0.8	Foreign debt	4.6
Net transfers	0.4	as % of GDP	61.9
Current account balance	-0.4	Debt service	
as % of GDP	-5.0	as % of export earnings	13.5

Principal exports[a]	*$m fob*	**Principal imports**[b]	*$m cif*
Ferro-nickel	221	Intermediate goods	602
Sugar	120	Capital goods	370
Cocoa	31	Consumer goods	361
Coffee	22	Fuels & energy	355

Main export destinations[a]	*% of total*	**Main origins of imports**[a]	*% of total*
USA	58.3	USA	45.5
EU	15.8	Venezuela	12.4
		Mexico	6.5
		Japan	5.2

Government

System Republic with president elected for 4 years by direct vote. Bicameral National Congress consisting of Senate and Chamber of Deputies.
Main political parties Social Christian Reformist Party, Dominican Revolutionary Party

Climate and topography

Tropical maritime with little seasonal variation in temperature. Shares island of Hispaniola with Haiti. Rugged highlands and mountains interspersed with fertile valleys.

People and society

Population m	7.5	% under 15	37.3
Pop. per sq km	153	% over 65	34
% urban	60	No. men per 100 women	103
% av. ann. growth 1987–92	2.2	Human Development Index	58.6
No. households m	...		

Life expectancy	*yrs*	**Education**	
Men	66	Spending as % of GDP	1.5
Women	70	Years of compulsory education	7
Crude birth rate	26	Adult literacy %	83
Crude death rate	7	Primary school enrolment %	73
Infant mortality		Secondary school enrolment %	74
per 1,000 live births	56	Tertiary education enrolment %	19

Workforce	*% of total*	**Consumer goods ownership**	
Services	39		*Pop. per*
Industry	15	Car	43.5
Agriculture	46	TV	11.9
% unemployed	...	Telephone	...

Ethnic groups	*% of total*	**Religious groups**	*% of total*
Mixed	73	Roman Catholic	95
White	16		
Black	11		

Tourism		**Health**	
Tourist arrivals m	1.5	Pop. per doctor	1,770
Tourist receipts $bn	0.8		

a 1991.
b 1989.

GRENADA

Grenada is a beautiful island where nothing much happens. Between 1979 and 1983, however, it was at the heart of a crisis involving the United States, Russia and Cuba.

History: four phases

Grenada became a British colony in 1783 and independent in 1974. Its first prime minister, Eric Gairy, was autocratic and a believer in flying saucers. In 1979 a small band of Marxist radicals led by Maurice Bishop of the New Jewel Movement seized power. Bishop formed close links with Cuba, jailed some opponents, censored the only newspaper, controlled the radio station and signed a pact to obtain a huge armoury of Soviet weapons. In the United States, the Reagan administration was horrified at the prospect of the establishment of a Cuban air base at the island's airport, which the Cubans were building.

The comrades disagree

After he lost a struggle for the leadership of his movement, Bishop was executed by the men who replaced him in 1983. Soon afterwards 1,900 American troops and 300 from the Organisation of Eastern Caribbean States invaded Grenada and ousted the new rulers. The invasion was immensely popular among the many islanders who had not supported either Bishop or his more radical successors. Nobody invited this force in, however; a letter from the governor-general, Sir Paul Scoon, asking for an intervention, which emerged afterwards, did not bear a date. A free election was held and won by centrists led by Herbert Blaize, who was subsequently replaced by Nicholas Brathwaite, a former UN official. However, promises of major post-invasion American investments came to nothing.

The economy: hopes for tourism

Total tourist arrivals rose from 198,000 in 1988 to about 290,000 in 1992. Exports of both nutmeg and mace, however, fell by five-sixths and cocoa exports fell by nearly half in the same period because of lower world prices and reduced harvests. A half-baked idea was being promoted for a return to growing bananas (which had been decimated by "black smut" disease) for the European market. A structural adjustment plan provides for cuts in government spending and in government debt. If successful, Grenada will be able to meet its international obligations in full. The plan made Mr Brathwaite unpopular.

Total area	340 sq km	% agricultural area	44
Capital	Saint George's	Highest point metres	Mount St. Catherine 840

The economy

GDP $m	210	GDP per head $	2,310
% av. ann. growth in real GDP 1987–92	3.9	GDP per head in purchasing power parity (USA=100)	...

Origins of GDP	*% of total*	**Components of GDP**	*% of total*
Agriculture	14	Private consumption	69
Industry	21	Public consumption	19
of which:		Investment	40
manufacturing	6	Exports	45
Services	65	Imports	77

Principal exports	*$m fob*	**Principal imports**[a]	*$m cif*
Bananas	2.8	Food	28
Cocoa	2.6	Mineral fuels	9
Nutmeg	2.1	Beverages & tobacco	2

Government

System Constitutional monarchy and parliamentary democracy with governor-general representing Queen Elizabeth II. Bicameral parliament consists of Senate and House of Representatives.

Main political parties National Democratic Congress, Grenada United Labour Party

Climate and topography

Tropical, but tempered by northeast trade winds. Mostly southerly of Windward Islands in Caribbean Sea. Volcanic in origin with central mountains.

People and society

Population	83,560	% under 15	35.2
Pop. per sq km	246	% over 65	6.6
% urban	...	No. men per 100 women	94
% av. ann. growth 1987–92	nil	No. households m	...
Human Development Index	78.7		

Ethnic groups	*% of total*	**Religious groups**	*% of total*
African	95	...	

a 1991.

GUADELOUPE

Regardless of the objections, sometimes violent, of a small minority of the black community, the Caribbean island of Guadeloupe is regarded as an integral part of France and is likely to remain so. It sends four representatives to the National Assembly and two to the Senate. The two most important figures on the island are the president of the autonomous General Council (a Guadeloupean) and the French prefect.

History: unhelpful violence

France has held Guadeloupe on and off since 1635. From a colony it became an Overseas Department in 1946 and gained more autonomy in 1983. Ten years later Guadeloupe looked like a quiet piece of France transferred to the tropics, administered by a contingent of French civil servants working for the prefect. The restaurants were full; the tourists poured in. The capital, Basse Terre, looked prosperous. It was not always so. In the 1980s several groups of dissidents, some violent and others non-violent, pressed for independence. The violent ones, led by the Armed Liberation Group, detonated bombs in hotels and government offices. Its political arm, like Sinn Fein in Northern Ireland, was the Popular Movement for Independent Guadeloupe. Although France pumps large sums into Guadeloupe every year, and its citizens who have jobs enjoy a standard of living approaching European levels, unemployment has been put as high as 45%.

The economy: more bananas

Guadeloupe runs a large trade deficit which France conveniently covers. About three-quarters of the island's exports – bananas, sugar and rum – go to France, which has tried to protect banana-growers from low-cost Latin American competition. Islanders are trying to diversify into crops such as pineapples. The government has tried to diversify the labour market too by promoting the construction of tourist hotels. Increasingly Guadeloupe depends on tourism. Two territories linked to it, Saint Martin (which shares an island with Dutch St Maarten) and Saint Barthélemy (known as St Barts), depend almost totally on tourism. As long as it is asked to do so, France will probably continue to spend its taxpayers' money on propping up Guadeloupe.

Total area	1,780 sq km	% agricultural area	36
Capital	Basse-Terre	Highest point metres	San Frière 1,484

Government

System Overseas department of France administered by a Conseil Général of 42 members and Regional Council of 39 members. Represented in the French National Assembly by 4 deputies and 2 senators.
Main political parties Rally for the Republic, Communist Party, Socialist Party

Climate and topography

Sub-tropical, with relatively high humidity, but tempered by trade winds. Basse-Terre is volcanic in origin with interior mountains. Grande-Terre is a low limestone formation.

People and society

Population	40,000	% under 15	27.1
Pop. per sq km	2.1	% over 65	7.8
% urban	...	No. men per 100 women	96
% av. ann. growth 1987–92	...	No. households m	...
Human Development Index	...		

Ethnic groups	*% of total*	**Religious groups**	*% of total*
Black or mixed	90	Roman Catholic	95
White	5	Hindu/pagan African	5
East Indian and other	5		

HAITI

Total area	27,750 sq km	Population	6.8m
GDP	$2.5bn	GDP per head	$380
Capital	Port-au-Prince	Other cities	Cap Haitien, Les Cayes, Jacmel

After the United States, Haiti was the first country in the Americas to rebel and obtain independence. Since then, the ex-slave republic has had a tormented history of coups, violence, poverty and oppression and little hope of an improvement.

History: permanently unstable

The rebellion, led by Toussaint L'Ouverture, began in 1791 in what was then the French colony of Saint-Domingue, where half a million slaves were exploited on plantations. After independence in 1804, the real trouble began. Jean-Jacques Dessalines broke up the sugar estates, declared himself emperor (like Napoleon) in 1805 and was assassinated in 1806. His successor, Henri Christophe, declared himself to be King Henry I, building a palace and the extraordinary Citadelle.

A break with the Spaniards

The Spaniards who lived in the east of the island rebelled against Haitian dominance and became independent, forming the Dominican Republic in 1844. From that year until the American marines arrived in 1915, Haiti was ruled by 22 dictators. A mulatto elite prospered while ex-slaves became poorer. In 1908 a president was blown up. In 1913 one was poisoned. In that year, after ordering the slaughter of 167 opponents, President Vilbrun Sam was impaled on the spikes of the French embassy's fence. American marines and sailors took control.

A quieter time

Under marine supervision, Stenio Vincent was elected president in 1930. But in 1934, after the marines were withdrawn, the masses went on a rampage. Vincent declared martial law and kept power until 1941. There followed a mulatto elitist, Elie Lescot (1941–1946), a black nationalist, Dumarsais Estime (1946–50), and a pragmatic black colonel, Paul Magloire (1950–56), who was one of Haiti's best presidents even if he squandered public funds.

Darkness and Duvalier

The 1957 election was won freely by a quiet doctor,

François (Papa Doc) Duvalier, who imposed a rule of terror and voodoo that lasted until he died in 1971. Thousands were killed, tortured or left to rot in jail. Discipline was maintained by thugs called Tontons Macoutes (bogeymen). The mulatto elite, the army and the church were sidelined. Duvalier was to superstitious Haitians one of the characters in the voodoo pantheon: Baron Samedi, an ominous undertaker-like figure who wears a black bowler hat. The situation improved under Jean-Claude (Baby Doc) Duvalier (1971–86), who encouraged American assembly industries to invest in Haiti, thus creating urgently needed jobs. But the corrupt Duvalierists kept power.

Politics: post-Duvalier

After Baby Doc was ousted in 1986 a general, Henri Namphy, took over. A year later a presidential election was aborted when Duvalierist gunmen ran amok. A subsequent election was rigged by General Namphy in favour of Leslie Manigat, an apparently compliant intellectual who unexpectedly opposed the army's smuggling operations and was deposed after six months. A free election in 1990 was won by a hugely popular leftist priest, Jean-Bertrand Aristide, who was unacceptable to the army and the elite and was ousted in 1992. In one notorious speech he implied support for killing his enemies by "necklacing" them with a burning tyre; he said he liked the smell of burning rubber. He was replaced, temporarily, in a wave of oppression by Marc Bazin, a former World Bank executive, as prime minister. The Organisation of American States slapped a trade embargo on Haiti. A painstaking agreement between Mr Aristide and the army with American and UN mediation to restore the ousted leader to the presidency was broken by the army in 1993.

The economy: disastrous

Haiti's agriculture, mainstay of the population, shrank as land became eroded. Some assembly industries, mostly in textiles, attracted to Haiti by Baby Doc, closed or left as a result of the trade embargo; no new investments came in. The people became desperate in the early 1990s. Thousands tried to reach the American mainland or the American military base at Guantanamo Bay, Cuba, in frail old boats, hoping to be allowed to go to Miami. But American Coast Guard cutters took most of the pathetic "boat people" back to Port-au-Prince, where their nightmare would begin again.

Total area	27,750 sq km	% agricultural area	51
Capital	Port-au-Prince	Highest point metres	Pic La Selle
Other cities	Cap Haitien,		2,680
	Les Cayes, Jacmel	Main rivers	Artibonite

The economy

GDP $bn	2.5	GDP per head $	380
% av. ann. growth in real GDP 1987–91	-0.7	GDP per head in purchasing power parity (USA=100)	5.5

Origins of GDP	*% of total*	**Components of GDP**[a]	*% of total*
Agriculture	...	Private[b] consumption	96
Industry	...	Public consumption	...
of which:		Investment	13
manufacturing	...	Exports	15
Services	...	Imports	-24

Structure of manufacturing

			% of total
Agric. & food processing	...	Other	...
Textiles & clothing	...	Av. ann. increase in industrial	
Machinery & transport	...	output 1987–92	...

Inflation and exchange rates

Consumer price 1993 av. ann. incr.	...	Gourdes per $ av. 1993	7.11
Av. ann. rate 1987–90	10.6%	Gourdes per ecu av. 1993	...

Balance of payments[a], reserves, aid and debt

			$bn
Visible exports fob	0.2	Capital balance	0.02
Visible imports fob	-0.3	Overall balance	-0.04
Trade balance	-0.1	Change in reserves	0.01
Invisible inflows	0.09	Level of reserves end Dec.	0.02
Invisible outflows	-0.2	Foreign debt	0.8
Net transfers	0.2	as % of GDP	28.8
Current account balance	-0.01	Debt service	
as % of GDP	-1.6	as % of export earnings	6.6

Principal exports	*$m fob*	**Principal imports**	*$m cif*
Manufactures	87	Food, beverages & tobacco	119
Coffee	18	Hydrocarbons	89
		Manufactures	52
		Machinery & transport equip.	27

Main export destinations	*% of total*	**Main origins of imports**	*% of total*
USA	76.7	USA	56.3
France	6.8	Netherlands Antilles	7.3
Italy	5.1	EU	16.9
Germany	4.6		

Government

System Republic, with bicameral legislature and executive president. President ousted in 1991 coup but still recognised by international community.

Main political parties National Front for Change and Democracy, Movement for the Installation of Democracy

Climate and topography

Tropical, semi-arid in lee of mountains. Shares island of Hispaniola with Dominican Republic.

People and society

Population m	6.8	% under 15	40.0
Pop. per sq km	244	% over 65	4.1
% urban	28	No. men per 100 women	97
% av. ann. growth 1987–92	2.0	Human Development Index	27.5
No. households m	...		

Life expectancy	*yrs*	**Education**	
Men	53	Spending as % of GDP	1.8
Women	55	Years of compulsory education	9
Crude birth rate	42	Adult literacy %	53
Crude death rate	15	Primary school enrolment %	44
Infant mortality		Secondary school enrolment %	19
per 1,000 live births	104	Tertiary education enrolment %	1

Workforce	*% of total*	**Consumer goods ownership**	
Services	44		*Pop. per*
Industry	6	Car	250.0
Agriculture	50	TV	200.0
% unemployed	...	Telephone	111.1

Ethnic groups	*% of total*	**Religious groups**	*% of total*
Black	95	Roman Catholic	80
Mulatto and European	5	Protestant	16

Tourism		**Health**	
Tourist arrivals m	0.1	Pop. per doctor	7,140
Tourist receipts $m	75		

a Fiscal year ending September 30th 1991.
b Includes government.

JAMAICA

Total area	10,990 sq km	Population	2.5m
GDP	$3.2bn	GDP per head	$1,340
Capital	Kingston	Other cities	Montego Bay, Spanish Town

Jamaica is the largest of the English-speaking islands of the Caribbean and has the largest population. It is a vigorous and well-established two-party democracy. But it has deep-seated social problems and has suffered several economic crises under weak governments. The government has adopted structural reforms which it hopes will pull it clear of its difficulties.

History: the populist and the patriarch

Jamaica was discovered in 1494 by members of the expedition led by Christopher Columbus. The British took the island over in 1655 and ruled it until Jamaica became independent in 1962. Until abolition in 1834 it was a slave-based economy producing sugar and some coffee for export. Sugar remained the basis of the economy for years. In the 1930s there were stirrings of independence led by Alexander Bustamante, a spell-binding orator who founded the Jamaica Labour Party (JLP) and his own trade union. Beneath his extravagant promises, however, Bustamante was a conservative. His long-lasting opponent was Norman Manley, a barrister who formed part, with several other West Indian leaders, of a Caribbean Fabian tradition rooted in the ideas of the London School of Economics. Regardless of the climate, Manley always wore a suit with waistcoat. He founded the centre-left People's National Party (PNP).

Politics: father and son

Between 1958 and 1962 the former British Caribbean islands tried to live together in the Federation of the West Indies. Bustamante, recognising that Jamaicans did not want be tied to "small islands", campaigned against it in a referendum. He won. The JLP had two terms in government (1962–67 and 1967–72). In 1972 Michael Manley, Norman's son, became prime minister. He nationalised some industries, increased subsidies and welfare payments and established good relations with Cuba. Finances went from bad to worse, and he suspended relations with the International Monetary Fund in 1979.

Enter Seaga

A year later the JLP, now led by the conservative Edward Seaga, won the general election. Mr Seaga restored relations with the IMF and became the Caribbean favourite of President Reagan. In 1983 he called a snap election which surprised Mr Manley and the PNP refused to take part; the JLP won every seat. Mr Seaga cut subsidies on food and fuel. He did not, however, privatise all government enterprises. In 1986–87 he had a dispute with the IMF over his expansionary spending programme, which the IMF wanted to rein in. An agreement led to deflation, which made Mr Seaga unpopular. Back came Mr Manley. But during his years in the wilderness he had taken a closer look at Fidel Castro's Cuba and concluded that the IMF had some good ideas which he proceeded to implement. He was succeeded in 1992 by P.J. Patterson, who followed the same line.

Society: law and order

This cheerful, easy-going society has acquired a culture of violence, encouraged by political parties which paid gangs to protect their interests. Violence is now hard to control in poor parts of Kingston, the capital, where the police are inefficient and, in some cases, corrupt. Crime in tourist areas, a problem in the 1970s, appeared to have abated in the 1990s.

The economy: diversified

Once a sugar monoculture, Jamaica now produces bananas, coffee, citrus fruit, onions, peppers and other vegetables as well as an excellent rum. It also produces large quantities of bauxite for aluminium, although the market is volatile. At times increases in output merely cushion losses when the price falls. Agriculture, bauxite and tourism fail to prevent a long-running trade deficit ($400m in 1992). After running at 6–25% between 1983 and 1990, inflation rose to 51% in 1991 and 77% in 1992. However, an effort was made in 1992 to cut government expenditure and to stabilise the Jamaican dollar, following its liberalisation in 1991, which led to a devaluation and made the country more competitive. After many years of current-account deficits, Jamaica had a surplus in 1992 and was in good standing with the IMF. The government also rescheduled debt servicing to creditor governments.

Total area	10,990 sq km	% agricultural area	43
Capital	Kingston	Highest point metres	Blue Mountain Peak 2,256
Other cities	Montego Bay, Spanish Town	Main rivers	Black

The economy

GDP $bn	3.2	GDP per head $	1,340
% av. ann. growth in real GDP 1987–90	3.3	GDP per head in purchasing power parity (USA=100)	16.6

Origins of GDP	*% of total*	**Components of GDP**	*% of total*
Agriculture	5	Private consumption	68
Industry	40	Public consumption	12
of which:		Investment	20
manufacturing	17	Exports	64
Services	56	Imports	-54

Structure of manufacturing

		% of total	
Agric. & food processing	...	Other	...
Textiles & clothing	...	Av. ann. increase in industrial	
Machinery & transport	...	output 1987–90	7.6

Inflation and exchange rates

Consumer price 1992 av. ann. incr.	77.3%	Jamaican $ per $ av. 1993	24.95
Av. ann. rate 1987–92	32.2%	Jamaican $ per ecu av. 1993	27.94

Balance of payments, reserves, aid and debt

			$bn
Visible exports fob	1.1	Capital balance	0.2
Visible imports fob	-1.5	Overall balance	0.3
Trade balance	-0.4	Change in reserves	-0.2
Invisible inflows	1.3	Level of reserves end Dec.[a]	0.1
Invisible outflows	-1.1	Foreign debt	4.3
Net transfers	0.3	as % of GDP	153.6
Current account balance	0.1	Debt service	
as % of GDP	3.7	as % of export earnings	24.8

Principal exports	*$m fob*	**Principal imports**	*$m cif*
Alumina	558	Fuel	291
Bauxite	113	Machinery & transport equip.	369
Sugar	91	Manufactured goods	285
Bananas	41	Chemicals	220

Main export destinations	*% of total*	**Main origins of imports**	*% of total*
USA	39.9	USA	52.6
UK	14.0	Venezuela	5.6
Germany	10.2	UK	5.3
Canada	9.6	Germany	4.6

Government

System Constitutional monarchy and parliamentary democracy with governor-general representing Queen Elizabeth II. Bicameral parliament consisting of Senate and House of Representatives. Both houses choose prime minister.

Main political parties People's National Party, Jamaica Labour Party

Climate and topography

Tropical. Hot and humid with temperate interior. Mostly mountains with narrow, irregular coastal plain.

People and society

Population m	2.5	% under 15	34.2
Pop. per sq km	225	% over 65	6.5
% urban	52	No. men per 100 women	97
% av. ann. growth 1987–92	1.0	Human Development Index	73.6
No. households m	...		

Life expectancy	*yrs*	**Education**	
Men	72	Spending as % of GDP	5.9
Women	76	Years of compulsory education	...
Crude birth rate	23	Adult literacy %	98
Crude death rate	6	Primary school enrolment %	94
Infant mortality		Secondary school enrolment %	60
per 1,000 live births	18	Tertiary education enrolment %	5

Workforce	*% of total*	**Consumer goods ownership**	
			Pop. per
Services	63		
Industry	12	Car	...
Agriculture	25	TV	7.7
% unemployed	...	Telephone	...

Ethnic groups	*% of total*	**Religious groups**	*% of total*
Black	76	Church of God	18
Afro-European	15	Baptist	10
East Indian	3	Anglican	7
White	3	Seventh-Day Adventist	7
		Other	58

Tourism		**Health**	
Tourist arrivals m	0.8	Pop. per doctor	2,040
Tourist receipts $bn	0.7		

a 1991.

MARTINIQUE

Like Guadeloupe, its sister French island, Martinique depends too much on the Paris government and its own bananas and sugar. Thanks to France its living standards are among the highest in the West Indies.

History: a brief bombing

Martinique has been ruled uneventfully by France since 1635. One of its few claims to fame is that it was the birthplace of Napoleon's Empress Josephine. In 1984, however, Martinique like Guadeloupe experienced attacks on government offices and the Empress Josephine Museum at Les Trois Ilets was destroyed by arson. The Caribbean Revolutionary Alliance was blamed. After these incidents, however, calm returned.

Politics: a looser connection

For centuries Martinique was ruled by a French governor. After the end of the second world war the ties were loosened though they still remained close. The island was administered by a prefect like any French department and had a regional council which was steadily given wider powers over the local economy in order, paradoxically, to discourage separatist pressure. After elections in 1988 and 1992 the council was run by a coalition of left-wing parties. Its president was Emile Capgras of the Martinique Progressive Party. Martinique sends four members to the French National Assembly and two to the Senate.

The economy: unbalanced

It is asking for trouble to erect a relatively high-wage society dependent on a distant country in a competitive region like the Caribbean. The danger is that Martinique and Guadeloupe price themselves out of the market. It is no accident that about 30% of Martinique's workforce is unemployed. Tourism does quite well, but high-cost bananas are threatened by more efficient Latin American producers and the world price of sugar has always been unpredictable. The main small industry (there are no large ones) makes rum. So far, France has been happy to subsidise Martinique to the hilt, modernise its infrastructure and send a small army of bureaucrats to run the administration. But for how long?

Total area	1,100 sq km	% agricultural area	48
Capital	Fort-de-France	Highest point metres	Montagne Pelée 1,396

Government

System Overseas department of France. Administered by a General Council of 45 members and Regional Council of 41 members, both directly elected. Represented in French National Assembly by 4 deputies and 2 senators.
Main political parties Rally for the Republic, Union of the Left, Union for French Democracy

Climate and topography

Tropical. Moderated by trade winds, with rainy season from June to October. Mountainous interior with indented coastline.

People and society

Population	370,000	% under 15	11.4
Pop. per sq km	336	% over 65	9.7
% urban	...	No. men per 100 women	94
% av. ann. growth 1987–92	1.1	No. households m	...
Human Development Index	...		

Ethnic groups	*% of total*	**Religious groups**	*% of total*
African and mixed	90	Roman Catholic	95
White	5	Hindu/pagan African	5
East Indian and other	5		

MONTSERRAT

Montserrat is a small island with a small population that remains a British Dependent Territory run by a governor sent from London. It has had a problem over "brass-plate banks" and alleged corruption.

History: uninterrupted stay

Montserrat was first settled by the British in 1632 and their stay has been uninterrupted. From 1871 to 1956 it was part of the Leeward Islands. It then became a British Dependent Territory.

Politics: money trouble

There is an Executive Council comprising the governor, the chief minister, the attorney-general and three other ministers, and a partly elected Legislative Council. In 1986 a dispute erupted over the inclusion of a casino in a tourism project. In 1992 the government cracked down on some councillors because of suspicions of bank fraud and alleged corruption. The British carried out an investigation of the "brass-plate" banks registered on the island and cracked down on some dubious ones. More than 300 offshore banks were closed, leaving only 21. An attempt was made to restore offshore banking under tighter supervision. But the chief minister, John Osborne of the People's Liberation Movement, resigned over allegations of corruption and was replaced, after an election, by Reuben Mead of the National Progressive Party. Mr Osborne was arrested. The government is now trying to "enhance" the island's reputation as an off-shore haven.

The economy: modest

The island's tiny GDP fell by 23.7% in 1991 but bounced back by 4% in 1992. Income from construction and tourism (out-of-the-way Montserrat specialises in the retiree market) has been weak but unemployment is only about 3% and inflation about 4%. Agriculture does well although only a relatively small amount of land is under cultivation, mainly for the local market. A sustained publicity drive may increase revenue from tourism, which accounts for roughly 15% of GDP. The island's trade deficit is covered mainly by remittances from abroad and British government assistance. Montserrat must learn to pay for itself in the world.

Total area	100 sq km	% agricultural area	30
Capital	Plymouth	Highest point metres	Chance Peak 915

The economy

GDP $m	537	GDP per head $	4,886
% av. ann. growth in real GDP 1985–92	...	GDP per head in purchasing power parity (USA=100)	...

Origins of GDP	*% of total*	**Components of GDP**	*% of total*
Agriculture	4	Private consumption	77
Industry	19	Public consumption	23
of which:		Investment	45
manufacturing	2	Exports	34
Services	77	Imports	-70

Government

System Dependent territory of the UK. Crown appoints governor. Unicameral Legislative Council consists of 7 elected and 2 civil service officials.
Main political parties National Progressive Party, People's Liberation Movement

Climate and topography

Tropical, with little daily or seasonal variations in temperature and rainfall. Volcanic island; mostly mountainous with a small coastal lowland.

People and society

Population	10,900	% under 15	33.3
Pop. per sq km	100	% over 65	nil
% urban	...	No. men per 100 women	100
% av. ann. growth 1987–92	nil	No. households m	...
Human Development Index	...		

Ethnic groups	*% of total*	**Religious groups**	*% of total*
Black	95	...	

NETH. ANTILLES

Scattered in the Caribbean, the Netherlands Antilles and Aruba are havens of racial peace and hotbeds of political bickering subsidised by the Dutch (at $145m a year).

History: a peaceful split

The islands had a history of piracy and plunder culminating in a long period of stability. The Netherlands Antilles included Aruba until 1986 when it gained a "status apart" en route to independence in 1996. Both territories remained part of the Netherlands. The Antilles now comprises Bonaire and Curaçao in the southern Caribbean close to Aruba off the Venezuelan coast, and Saba, St Eustatius and St Maarten (half-shared with France) in the northern Caribbean near Puerto Rico.

Politics: no Dutch treats, please

The territories are ruled by governors or vice-governors with local councils having a wide degree of autonomy. After riots over unemployment in 1969, the Dutch government started talking about independence; the islanders preferred to stay Dutch. Since then, bickering about the various islands' interests has continued. The election in February 1994 was won by the new, business-oriented Antillean Restructuring Party, led by Miguel Pourier, campaigning to maintain the unity of the Antilles. St Maarten was a worry: its government appeared to have been taken over by drug-traffickers. In 1992 the Dutch intervened and took all financial decisions; the political boss was subsequently arrested.

The economy: restructuring needed

Aruba's economy was badly hit in 1985 when its oil refinery closed with a loss of 60% of the island's income. It has been leased to Venezuela but needs extensive repairs. Tourism flourishes but the big dry docks do not. Willemstad is a busy centre for private trading. Aruba and the Netherlands Antilles both run big budget deficits. The debt of the Antilles is $1.42 billion; that of Aruba $228m. The economies of both the Antilles and Aruba are in urgent need of restructuring. Dutch aid now goes only to development projects; there is no budget assistance.

Total area	960 sq km	% agricultural area	8
Capital	Willemstad	Highest point metres	375

The economy

GDP $bn	1.3[a]	GDP per head $	7,058
% av. ann. growth in real GDP 1987–92	...	GDP per head in purchasing power parity (USA=100)	...

Origins of GDP	*% of total*	**Components of GDP**	*% of total*
Agriculture	1	Private consumption	61
Industry	4	Public consumption	16
of which:		Investment	17
manufacturing	7	Exports	31
Services	58	Imports	-29

Government

System Part of kingdom of Netherlands. Full autonomy in internal affairs obtained in 1986. The Dutch monarch is represented by a governor-general. Unicameral legislature.

Main political parties National People's Party (Curaçao), Patriotic Union of Bonaire

Climate and topography

Tropical but tempered by north-east trade winds. Curaçao and Bonaire are in the Leeward Islands, about 100km north of Venezuela. St Maarten and St Eustatius are in the Windward Islands, about 800km to the north-east.

People and society

Population	170,000	% under 15	27.0
Pop. per sq km	177	% over 65	7.4
% urban	...	No. men per 100 women	95
% av. ann. growth 1987–92	nil	No. households m	...
Human Development Index	...		

Ethnic groups	*% of total*	**Religious groups**	*% of total*
African and mixed	85	...	

Aruba

Total area	193 sq km	Population	60,000
GDP	$1.1bn	GDP per head	$15,674

PUERTO RICO

Total area	9,104 sq km	Population	3.6m
GDP	$23.6bn	GDP per head	$6,610
Capital	San Juan	Other cities	Bayamon, Ponce

Puerto Rico is a hybrid and a paradox. It is both a democracy and a colony. It is part of the United States yet it has no representation in Congress and cannot vote in presidential elections. Many of its citizens, whose first language is Spanish, vehemently express the desire for Puerto Rico to become a state of the union; others equally vehemently demand independence. In the middle is an ambivalent majority which prefers the best of both worlds: to continue the present arrangement with some refinements. This arrangement is that Puerto Rico is (in English) a "Commonwealth" and (in Spanish) a "Free Associated State" of the United States. As long as Puerto Ricans fail to send a clearer message to the American Congress about their preference, Congress will leave them as they are.

History: from Spain to America

Puerto Rico was discovered by Christopher Columbus in 1493 and the island became a Spanish possession. Sugar was first planted in 1515; African slaves arrived three years later. Puerto Rico remained Spanish until 1898 when, in the settlement at the end of the Spanish-American war, it was ceded with Cuba to America. It has remained an American possession ever since. From 1898 to 1900 it was ruled by American governors. The 1900 Foraker Act gave it an elected House of Delegates. In 1917 the Jones Act granted Puerto Ricans American citizenship and an elected Senate. In 1922 the Nationalist Party was born, calling for independence.

Enter Luis Munoz Marin

In 1944 the man who was to dominate Puerto Rican politics for a generation, Luis Munoz Marin, founded the Popular Democratic Party (PPD). In 1947, after Congress allowed them to be elected, he became the first governor. Munoz Marin started an economic development programme based on self-help called Operation Bootstrap. The island's status as a Free Associated State or Commonwealth was confirmed in 1953 after a favourable plebiscite and the United Nations accepted it a year later as a self-governing territory. However, the UN's General Assembly allowed a special committee to study the island's colonial status and gave a hearing to *independentistas.* Munoz Marin retired in 1964 but his heritage endured: another plebiscite on the island's status in 1967 resulted in a 60% endorsement of the Free Associated State against 38% for statehood.

Politics: an atmosphere of indecision

After Munoz Marin, lesser politicians held the governorship and called either for a vague "culmination" of the island's status granting it more autonomy or for statehood. Nobody was happy with the status quo. It was not surprising: without prior consultation, Congress abolished the island's food-stamp programme and converted it into a block grant amounting to less money; it abolished federally funded training programmes; and, in President Reagan's Caribbean Basin Initiative, it extended to some Caribbean islands the tariff privileges in sales to the United States that had been enjoyed by Puerto Rico alone.

However, in another referendum in 1993, voters confirmed their preference for Commonwealth status, but by a narrower margin than in 1967: 48% for no change, 46% for statehood and 4% for independence. It was likely that the numbers of those favouring statehood would grow, even if this meant they would have to pay their full federal taxes for the first time. President Bush thought statehood was the island's best solution and said so. What Congress would make of the idea of adding a Spanish-speaking state to the Union is another matter.

The economy: tied to America

Although it is relatively well off by Caribbean standards, Puerto Rico is poor by American standards, and 2m islanders have emigrated to the United States (no visa required; they are already American citizens). To boost industry, section 936 of the American tax code makes profits earned in Puerto Rico free of tax for American multinationals. Many of these companies, especially those in pharmaceuticals, have abandoned the continental United States for Puerto Rico's cheap labour and tax-free status, to the fury of American unions. Apart from pharmaceuticals, Puerto Rican industry comprises chemicals, electrical machinery, refining and food products. Agriculture is devoted mainly to coffee, plantains, yams, bananas, taniers and pigeon-peas. Puerto Rico has a large and healthy tourism industry, which finds favour with hundreds of thousands of Americans every year.

Total area	9,104 sq km	% agricultural area	58
Capital	San Juan	Highest point metres	Cerro de
Other cities	Bayamon, Ponce		Punta 1,338

The economy

GDP $bn	23.6	GDP per head $	6,610
% av. ann. growth in real GDP 1987–92	...	GDP per head in purchasing power parity (USA=100)	49.3

Origins of GDP	*% of total*	**Components of GDP**	*% of total*
Agriculture	1	Private consumption	64
Industry	41	Public consumption	15
of which:		Investment	16
manufacturing	39	Exports	76
Services	57	Imports	...

Structure of manufacturing

			% of total
Agric. & food processing	15	Other	62
Textiles & clothing	5	Av. ann. increase in industrial	
Machinery & transport	18	output 1987–92	...

Inflation and exchange rates[a]

Consumer price 1993 av. ann. incr.	...	per $ av. 1993	...
Av. ann. rate 1987–93	...	per ecu av. 1993	...

Balance of payments, reserves, aid and debt

			$bn
Visible exports fob	21.8	Capital balance	...
Visible imports fob	-14.8	Overall balance	...
Trade balance	7.0	Change in reserves	...
Invisible inflows	...	Level of reserves end Dec. 1993	...
Invisible outflows	...	Foreign debt	10.0
Net transfers	...	as % of GDP	40.3
Current account balance	...	Debt service	
as % of GDP	...	as % of export earnings	...

Main export destinations	*% of total*	**Main origins of imports**	*% of total*
Mainland USA	88.3	Mainland USA	68.8

Government

System Commonwealth associated with United States. Governor is directly elected every 4 years. Bicameral legislature comprising Senate and House of Representatives. Represented in US Congress by a Resident Commissioner.

Main political parties National Republican Party, Popular Democratic Party

Climate and topography

Tropical marine with little variation in temperature. Mountainous with coastal plain in north.

People and society

Population m	3.6	% under 15	26.1
Pop. per sq km	393	% over 65	10.4
% urban	...	No. men per 100 women	95
% av. ann. growth 1987–92	0.9	Human Development Index	...
No. households m	...		

Life expectancy	*yrs*	**Education**	
Men	70	Spending as % of GDP	...
Women	78	Years of compulsory education	9
Crude birth rate	17	Adult literacy %	90
Crude death rate	8	Primary school enrolment %	...
Infant mortality		Secondary school enrolment %	...
per 1,000 live births	14	Tertiary education enrolment %	...

Workforce	*% of total*	**Consumer goods ownership**	
Services	...		*Pop. per*
Industry	...	Car	...
Agriculture	...	TV	...
% unemployed	...	Telephone	...

Ethnic groups	*% of total*	**Religious groups**	*% of total*
Hispanic	98	Roman Catholic	85
		Protestant and other	15

Tourism		**Health**	
Tourist arrivals m	2.6	Pop. per doctor	...
Tourist receipts $bn	1.4		

a Currency is US dollar.

ST. KITTS AND NEVIS

The two islands of St Kitts and Nevis live quietly in the eastern Caribbean under a relatively competent and cautious government. The economy has grown steadily. There have, however, been some shake-ups.

History: stable progress

St Kitts (officially known as St Christopher) and Nevis were ruled by Britain as a colony from 1816. They joined the unsuccessful West Indies Federation (1958–62) and, after an interim period, became independent as a member of the Commonwealth with Queen Elizabeth as monarch, represented by a governor-general, in 1983.

Politics: worrying

After 28 years of government by the Labour Party, an election in 1980 was won by the People's Action Movement and the Nevis Reformation Party. Dr Kennedy Simmonds became prime minister. One member of his government was accused of money-laundering and another was dismissed without explanation. The general election in 1993 led to a political crisis. Both the ruling People's Action Movement and the opposition Labour Party won four seats in the 11-seat parliament. The Concerned Citizens' Movement (CCM) won two and the Nevis Reformation Party (NRP) gained one. The CCM decided it would not form a six-seat majority coalition with either the CCM or the Labour Party. So a minority five-seat coalition was formed by Dr Simmonds with the NRP. The CCM then said it would be "impartial" and Labour remained in opposition.

The economy: quite positive

Tourist arrivals increased from 123,000 in 1988 to 137,000 in 1992. New hotels have been built and the tourism industry is prospering. Agricultural output, particularly of sugar, tomatoes, carrots, cabbages, sweet potatoes, yams, groundnuts and onions, also increased. Sugar, which provides 2,500 jobs and roughly 40% of export earnings, can only be competitive if it expands through new investments. But the industry is heavily indebted and would find it difficult to borrow more. It remains a hostage to the fickle fortunes of the world sugar market. An attempt has been made to diversify into small factories making shoes, clothing and electronics.

Total area	269 sq km	% agricultural area	42
Capital	Basseterre	Highest point metres	Mount Misery 1,155

The economy

GDP $m	181	GDP per head $	3,990
% av. ann. growth in real GDP 1987–92	5.3	GDP per head in purchasing power parity (USA=100)	...

Origins of GDP	*% of total*	**Components of GDP**	*% of total*
Agriculture	...	Private consumption	65
Industry	...	Public consumption	18
of which:		Investment	56
manufacturing	...	Exports	51
Services	...	Imports	-90

Government

System Constitutional monarchy and parliamentary democracy with governor-general representing Queen Elizabeth II. Unicameral House of Assembly consists of 11 elected members and 3 appointed senators.

Main political parties People's Action Movement, Labour Party, Concerned Citizens' Movement, Nevis Reformation Party

Climate and topography

Sub-tropical, tempered by constant sea breezes. Little seasonal variation in temperature. Rainy season from May to November. Volcanic terrain with mountainous interior. Located 320 km southeast of Puerto Rico.

People and society

Population	40,000	% under 15	30.0
Pop. per sq km	149	% over 65	15.0
% urban	41	No. men per 100 women	90
% av. ann. growth 1987–92	nil	No. households m	...
Human Development Index	69.7		

Ethnic groups	*% of total*	**Religious groups**	*% of total*
Black African	95	...	

ST. LUCIA

Under John Compton, one of the elder statesmen of the Caribbean, St Lucia is doing quite well. The Caribbean Development Bank praises the government's "tight expenditure controls, careful cash-flow management and efficient tax collections". St Lucia has a problem, however: its dependence on bananas.

History: Compton triumphant

After 200 years of disagreement with the French, St Lucia was ceded to Britain in 1814. It formed part of the Windward Islands until 1959 and then part of the West Indies Federation until 1962. After that, it grew more autonomous by stages until it reached independence with Mr Compton, leader of the United Workers' Party, as prime minister in 1979. The opposition Labour Party won the election in the same year but lost the next one, in 1982, amid charges of corruption. Mr Compton bounced back.

Politics: a new era

In 1992 at the start of another five-year term of office, Mr Compton introduced four young politicians into his cabinet and indicated that he would step down before the end of his five years. The favourite to succeed him was Micky Pilgrim, formerly of the Labour Party, who had switched sides.

The economy: bananas still dominant

Apart from tourism, St Lucia relies on bananas as a money-earner. The world price has been weakening and future access to the European Union market is being challenged by lower-cost Latin American producers. Nevertheless, output was up by 30% in 1992. Prices slipped in 1993 and early 1994, provoking opposition-backed demonstrations by poor, small-scale banana-growers. In 1994 the heavily indebted St Lucia Banana Growers' Association, a government-sponsored co-operative which pays subsidies to farmers when the price is low, was placed in receivership. Coconuts also suffered from lower prices but farmers produced more breadfruit, plantains and mangoes. Tourist arrivals rose by 27% in 1991 and about 15% in 1992, due to skilful selling of St Lucia as an upmarket destination. The budget was usually in surplus and the foreign debt, though large and growing, was mostly long-term and sustainable. Small manufacturing has been hurt by weak American demand but was expected to perk up as the recession ended.

Total area	620 sq km	% agricultural area	33
Capital	Castries	Highest point metres	Mount Gimie 959

The economy

GDP $m	453	GDP per head $	2,900
% av. ann. growth in real GDP 1985–92	...	GDP per head in purchasing power parity (USA=100)	...

Government

System Constitutional monarchy and parliamentary democracy with governor-general representing Queen Elizabeth II. Bicameral parliament consists of Senate and House of Assembly. Senate is appointed by governor-general.

Main political parties United Workers' Party, St Lucia Labour Party

Climate and topography

Tropical, moderated by northeast trade winds. Rainy season from May to August. Volcanic and mountainous with some broad fertile valleys. Located 700 km southeast of Puerto Rico.

People and society

Population	14,000	% under 15	41.3
Pop. per sq km	23	% over 65	6.0
% urban	...	No. men per 100 women	92
% av. ann. growth 1987–92	nil	No. households m	...
Human Development Index	72.0		

Ethnic groups	*% of total*	**Religious groups**	*% of total*
Black African	90	Roman Catholic	90
Mixed	6	Protestant	7
East Indian	3	Anglican	3

ST. VINCENT

St Vincent and the tiny Grenadine islands are a beautiful collection of Caribbean islands with lovely beaches. But they depend excessively on bananas for economic survival.

History: The rise of James Mitchell

St Vincent and the Grenadines became British possessions in the 18th century as part of the Windward Islands. They came under the unsuccessful West Indies Federation before evolving to independence in 1979. In the pre-independence days of 1972, with the two main parties holding six parliamentary seats each, James Mitchell, the sole independent, parlayed his position into being named premier. He lasted two years; the government fell over a dispute between Mr Mitchell and his coalition ally. The opposition St Vincent Labour Party won in 1974 and again in 1979 but Mr Mitchell's New Democratic Party, capitalising on the government's unpopularity, won the 1984 election. He became prime minister, winning re-election in 1994.

The economy: vulnerable

St Vincent's efforts to diversify out of bananas had not, by the early 1990s, achieved any notable success. The islands were hampered by having a relatively unskilled labour force and a high minimum wage. Their only niche product was arrowroot, of which the islands are the world leader. The sugar industry closed in 1985. Manufacturing was depressed following the closure of three offshore firms in 1989 and 1990. An industrial estate at Camden Park had vacancies and an attempt was made to accommodate small-scale indigenous producers.

Government revenues were lower than predicted in the early 1990s but the government exercised fiscal prudence. St Vincent runs a manageable trade deficit ($42m in 1992) and a current-account deficit ($20m). The external public debt in 1992 was $66m. Inflation was running at about 4%. GDP growth is healthy, averaging about 7% a year from 1988 to 1992.

A number of hotels and resorts are being built and a $55m airport on Bequia, the largest of the Grenadines, was opened in 1991. It was named after Mr Mitchell, the parliamentary representative for the Grenadines and a resident of Bequia.

Total area	340 sq km	% agricultural area	56
Capital	Kingstown	Highest point metres	Mount Saifrière 1,234

The economy

GDP $m	198.7	GDP per head $	1,655
% av. ann. growth in real GDP 1987–92	6.4	GDP per head in purchasing power parity (USA=100)	...

Origins of GDP	*% of total*	**Components of GDP**[a]	*% of total*
Agriculture	18	Private consumption	80
Industry	25	Public consumption	21
of which:		Investment	36
manufacturing	9	Exports	84
Services	57	Imports	-104

Principal exports	*$m fob*	**Principal imports**	*$m cif*
Bananas	36	...	
Flour	8		

Government

System Constitutional monarchy and parliamentary democracy with governor-general representing Queen Elizabeth II. Unicameral House of Assembly consists of 15 elected members and 6 appointed senators.
Main political parties New Democratic Party, St Vincent Labor Party

Climate and topography

Tropical with little seasonal variation in temperature. Rainy season from May to November. Volcanic, mountainous group of islands in Lesser Antilles.

People and society

Population	107,350	% under 15	34.6
Pop. per sq km	324	% over 65	5.6
% urban	27	No. men per 100 women	95
% av. ann. growth 1987–92	nil	No. households m	...
Human Development Index	70.9		

Ethnic groups	*% of total*	**Religious groups**	*% of total*
...		...	

a 1990.

TRINIDAD & TOBAGO

Total area	5,128 sq km	Population	1.3m
GDP	$5bn	GDP per head	$3,940
Capital	Port of Spain	Other cities	San Fernando, Arima

Trinidad and Tobago, the most industrialised of the Caribbean islands, is an untidy country full of difficulties ranging from the low world price of oil (which accounts for 23% of GDP) to the daunting size of its $2.2 billion foreign debt.

History: Williams showed the way

Trinidad was discovered in 1498 by a Spanish expedition led by Christopher Columbus and ruled by Spain until it was seized by the British in 1797. It was transferred to British sovereignty three years later. Nearby Tobago was ruled by France until 1763 when it was ceded to Britain. The islands lived in tranquillity under the British until the second world war when rumblings in favour of independence began. The leader was Dr Eric Williams, a distinguished intellectual who headed the People's National Movement (PNM). Williams, like Norman Manley in Jamaica, became a patriarch of the Caribbean. Trinidad was part of the unsuccessful experiment in federation in 1958–61. When Jamaica opted to leave, so did Trinidad. With Williams as prime minister, Trinidad became independent in 1962. He stayed in office until his death in 1981.

The good days

These were the good days, when Trinidadians enjoyed the pleasures of being a well-to-do oil-producer. But Williams's successor, the unexciting George Chambers (1981–86), tried to contain inflation through wage restraint and became unpopular. He was succeeded by the opposition National Alliance for Reconstruction (NAR), led by A.N.R. Robinson, which won 33 of the 36 seats in parliament. Mr Robinson published a report which alleged that five magistrates, two cabinet ministers and 53 policemen had trafficked in or used drugs.

The attempted coup

In 1990 114 Jamaat-al-Muslimeen extremists kidnapped Mr Robinson and most of his cabinet and held them hostage for five days. The extremists were caught and jailed but released by the High Court in July 1992 on the ground that the pardon given to them to save Mr Robinson's life and obtain his release, though under duress, was still valid. After being released, the coup leader, Abu Bakr, declined to apologise. Mr Robinson lost prestige and, in an election in 1991, his NAR won only two of the 36 parliamentary seats. The PNM, now led by Patrick Manning, took 21 and the United National Congress (UNC) 13.

Society: an unusual ethnic make-up

Trinidad has a complex ethnic make-up. The majority black population are descendants of ex-slaves who had been transported forcibly to Trinidad to work on the plantations. There are also large numbers of Indians descended from indentured labourers plus a small Chinese and European (mainly British) population.

The economy: a volatile blend

As the world oil price has slipped, so has Trinidad. GDP contracted for eight consecutive years until 1990. There was a fragile recovery in 1990 and 1991 but a slight decline in 1992. Reduced revenues from oil coupled with lower-than-anticipated production levels and a reduced refinery business made it difficult for Trinidad to service its foreign debt, which had already been twice rescheduled. But it was doing so in 1992, when the bill was $628m, with recourse to international borrowing and privatisation of state enterprises making fertilisers and urea. Nonetheless, foreign-exchange reserves fell in the first quarter of 1992 to a negative $119m. Reforms made at the behest of the World Bank and the IMF, including the abolition of quotas and reduction of import tariffs, opened up the economy to a wave of imports. Local businesses said 8,000 jobs could be lost; others said this was an exaggeration. The trade surplus, fuelled by oil exports, fell sharply in 1992.

Uncertain future

The government established an industrial park at Point Lisas, which was a success, and was planning a second one. Sugar, handled by the state monopoly Caroni, continued to contribute to the economy, selling in the protected markets of the United States and European Union. But output has tended to decline over the years. Trinidad also produces coffee and, increasingly, citrus fruits. With high unemployment and a flat economy, however, Trinidad's future is uncertain.

Total area	5,130 sq km	% agricultural area	33
Capital	Port-of-Spain	Highest point metres	Cerro Aripo
Other cities	San Fernando, Arima		940

The economy

GDP $bn	5.0	GDP per head $	3,940
% av. ann. growth in real GDP 1987–91	-0.1	GDP per head in purchasing power parity (USA=100)	37.9

Origins of GDP	*% of total*	**Components of GDP**	*% of total*
Agriculture	3	Private consumption	59
Industry	39	Public consumption	15
of which:		Investment	18
manufacturing	9	Exports	41
Services	58	Imports	-33

Structure of manufacturing

			% of total
Agric. & food processing	...	Other	...
Textiles & clothing	...	Av. ann. increase in industrial	
Machinery & transport	...	output 1987–92	3.8

Inflation and exchange rates

Consumer price 1993 av. ann. incr.	10.8%	Trinidad $ per $ av. 1993	5.35
Av. ann. rate 1987–93	10.0%	Trinidad $ per ecu av. 1993	5.99

Balance of payments, reserves, aid and debt

			$bn
Visible exports fob	1.7	Capital balance	-0.1
Visible imports fob	-1.0	Overall balance	-0.1
Trade balance	0.7	Change in reserves	-0.2
Invisible inflows	0.5	Level of reserves end Dec.	0.2
Invisible outflows	-1.0	Foreign debt	2.3
Net transfers	-0.01	as % of GDP	46.0
Current account balance	0.1	Debt service	
as % of GDP	2.3	as % of export earnings	25.2

Principal exports	*$bn fob*	**Principal imports**	*$bn cif*
Mineral fuels	1.2	Machinery & transport equip.	0.4
Chemicals	0.3	Manufactured goods	0.3
Manufactured goods	0.2	Mineral fuel	0.1
Food	0.1	Food & animals	0.1

Main export destinations	*% of total*	**Main origins of imports**	*% of total*
USA	47.0	USA	41.4
Caricom	13.0	Venezuela	9.7
Central & South America	8.5	UK	7.8
EU	5.4	Other EU	7.8

Government

System Parliamentary democracy. President elected by bicameral parliament which consists of a Senate and House of Representatives.

Main political parties People's National Movement, United National Congress, National Alliance for Reconstruction

Climate and topography

Tropical with rainy season from June to December. Mostly plains with some hills and low mountains. Located 11 km north of Venezuela.

People and society

Population m	1.3	% under 15	33.9
Pop. per sq km	246	% over 65	5.5
% urban	69	No. men per 100 women	97
% av. ann. growth 1987–92	0.8	Human Development Index	87.7
No. households m	...		

Life expectancy	*yrs*	**Education**	
Men	68	Spending as % of GDP	4.1
Women	73	Years of compulsory education	...
Crude birth rate	21	Adult literacy %	...
Crude death rate	6	Primary school enrolment %	90
Infant mortality		Secondary school enrolment %	80
per 1,000 live births	17	Tertiary education enrolment %	6

Workforce	*% of total*	**Consumer goods ownership**	
			Pop. per
Services	49		
Industry	41	Car	4.8
Agriculture	10	TV	3.3
% unemployed	...	Telephone	5.7

Ethnic groups	*% of total*	**Religious groups**	*% of total*
Black	43	Roman Catholic	32
East Indian	40	Hindu	24
Mixed	14	Anglican	14
White	1	Muslim	6
Chinese	1		

Tourism		**Health**	
Tourist arrivals m	0.2	Pop. per doctor	940
Tourist receipts $m	95		

TURKS & CAICOS IS.

The 30-odd Turks and Caicos Islands are small and the population is tiny but Grand Turk, the capital, has seen some scandalous times.

History: a lot of arrests

The British overrode French and Spanish claims to the islands in 1766 when a residential British agent was appointed. The islands were administered by the British from Jamaica from 1874 to 1959, after which they were ruled directly from London by a governor. A pro-independence party, the People's Democratic Movement, won an election to the Legislative Council in 1976 and planned to press for independence after winning the next one in 1980. But it lost to Norman Saunders's Progressive National Party, which won again in 1984.

Power corrupted, however. Mr Saunders was arrested in Miami in 1985 on drugs charges. Nathaniel Francis took over as chief minister. A year later Mr Francis and two other ministers resigned following publication of a report alleging arson among other things. The report said two opposition members were unfit for public office. The attorney-general was subsequently deported.

Britain wakes up

In 1986 the governor dissolved the government and the Executive Council, and ruled through a special Advisory Council of which he was chairman. In 1988 the old system returned and an election brought Oswald Skippings to power as chief minister. He was replaced after an election in 1991 by Washington Misick.

The economy: tourism, fish and banks

Tourism employs at least 2,000 islanders. Fishermen export lobsters, conch and conch shells. At least 10,600 offshore companies display their "brass plates" in Cockburn Town. The prospects are for an increase in tourism, especially on the island of Providenciales. The government wants to balance this with growth on the other larger island, Grand Turk.

Total area	430 sq km	% agricultural area	2
Capital	Grand Turk	Highest point metres	76

The economy

GDP $m	80.8	GDP per head $	6,413
% av. ann. growth in real GDP 1987–92	...	GDP per head in purchasing power parity (USA=100)	...

Origins of GDP	*% of total*	**Components of GDP**	*% of total*
Agriculture	7	Private consumption	...
Industry	17	Public consumption	...
of which:		Investment	...
manufacturing	1	Exports	...
Services	76	Imports	...

Principal exports	*$m fob*	**Principal imports**[a]	*$m cif*
Lobsters	4	Manufactured goods	26
		Food, drink & tobacco	11
		Fuels	4

Government

System British dependent territory with governor. Unicameral Legislative Council consists of 3 members from Executive Council, 13 elected and 2 appointed members.

Main political parties People's Democratic Movement, Progressive National Party

Climate and topography

Tropical marine climate moderated by trade winds. Sunny and relatively dry. 30 islands, eight inhabited. Low flat limestone with extensive marshes and mangrove swamps.

People and society

Population	12,700	% under 15	...
Pop. per sq km	30	% over 65	...
% urban	...	No. men per 100 women	...
% av. ann. growth 1987–92	nil	No. households m	...
Human Development Index	...		

Ethnic groups	*% of total*	**Religious groups**	*% of total*
Black African	95	Baptist	41
		Methodist	19
		Anglican	18
		Seventh-Day Adventist	2

a 1990.

VIRGIN ISLANDS (UK)

The 50-odd British Virgin Islands (BVI) and their population are dedicated to tourists and to registering foreign companies.

History: neglect and poverty

Christopher Columbus discovered the islands in 1493 on his way to Puerto Rico and called them "the 11,000 Virgins" after St Ursula and her legendary 11,000 martyred companions. Control was contested in the 18th century by Spain, Holland and Britain, which eventually established constitutional government in 1773. Small and inconsequential, the British Virgins suffered neglect and poverty throughout the 19th century.

Politics: a difficult relationship

Internal self-government came in 1967 and the first chief minister was H. Lavity Stoutt, who was re-elected in 1979 and 1986. Compared with the American Virgin Islands, the BVI are a backwater. A wish to avoid dependence on the United States has persuaded the BVI that its best interest lies in a continuing relationship with distant Britain, which provides a governor and uncomfortably insists, from time to time, on certain rules being respected. The relationship between strong-minded Mr Stoutt and British governors has been at times prickly.

The economy: tourists and companies

The islands have aimed for upmarket tourism, with luxury hotels scattered along the islands' coves and long beaches, and the yacht market. Company registration has boomed. In 1992 about 1,000 international companies were registered every month. The fees amounted to about a third of government income. The difficult British were looking into possible irregularities.

A spur to construction

Public works (the government building, a community college and additions to the port) and tourism developments have given a spur to the construction industry.

Total area	150 sq km	% agricultural area	60
Capital	Road Town	Highest point metres	Mount Sage 543

Government

System British dependent territory with governor. Legislative Council consists of Attorney-General and 9 elected members.

Main political parties United Party, Virgin Islands Party

Climate and topography

Sub-tropical and humid, but moderated by trade winds. Eastern extremity of Greater Antilles chain. 40 islands, of which 15 are inhabited. A mixture of flat coral islands and hilly volcanic islands.

People and society

Population	12,550	% under 15	...
Pop. per sq km	84	% over 65	...
% urban	...	No. men per 100 women	...
% av. ann. growth 1987–92	...	No. households m	...
Human Development Index	...		

Ethnic groups	*% of total*	**Religious groups**	*% of total*
Black	90	Methodist	45
		Anglican	21
		Church of God	7
		Seventh-Day Adventist	5
		Baptist	4

VIRGIN ISLANDS (US)

There are three American Virgin Islands: St Croix, St Thomas and St John. The islanders concentrate on tourism, which provides 70% of employment and of GDP.

History: the Danish West Indies

The islands were discovered by Christopher Columbus in 1493. By 1596 the indigenous population had been killed or had died of imported diseases. Danes settled in the islands in 1672 and remained there, in what was known as the Danish West Indies, until 1917, when the islands were sold to the United States for $25m. The islanders were given American citizenship in 1927, universal suffrage in 1936, an elected governor in 1970 and an elected delegate to the House of Representatives (who may vote in committee but not in the House) in 1973. There is a local legislature.

Politics: dominant Democrats

The Democratic Party's grip on the governorship ended in 1974 when the leader of a splinter group, Cyril King, was elected. He was succeeded on his death in 1978 by his lieutenant-governor, Juan Luis, who was elected in his own right in 1982. The Democrats returned to power in 1986 when Alexander Farrelly was elected governor. Mr Farrelly was re-elected in 1990.

The economy: sun and rum

The principal industries are tourism, rum, alumina, an oil refinery (one of the world's biggest) and some perfumes. International financial services are steadily expanding. The standard of living is more or less on a par with America's. Although there are many hotels, much of the tourism business is directed to the frequent visits of free-spending passengers in cruise ships (roughly 1,000 a year) and also in selling duty-free goods to visitors returning to the mainland. The islands are visited by roughly 1m tourists a year. The islanders depend heavily on their links to the United States. These links are direct, by air and freighter, but also via neighbouring Puerto Rico. The islands are much more lively and dynamic than the more unspoilt British Virgin Islands to the east, which have a much smaller population.

Total area	352 sq km	% agricultural area	47
Capital	Charlotte Arnalie	Highest point metres	Crown Mountain 474

Government

System Organised, unincorporated territory of the United States, administered by Department of the Interior. Unicameral Senate composed of 15 directly elected Senators.

Main political parties Democratic Party, Independent Citizen's Movement, Republican Party

Climate and topography

Sub-tropical with relatively low humidity and little seasonal variation in temperature. Rainy season from May to November. Groups of islands lying about 90 km from Puerto Rico. Mostly hilly with little level land.

People and society

Population	98,940	% under 15	32.7
Pop. per sq km	281	% over 65	5.5
% urban	...	No. men per 100 women	91
% av. ann. growth 1987–92	nil	No. households m	...
Human Development Index	...		

Ethnic groups	*% of total*	**Religious groups**	*% of total*
Black	80	Baptist	42
White	15	Roman Catholic	34
		Episcopalian	17

Part IV

SOUTH AMERICA COUNTRY PROFILES

126 Argentina
134 Bolivia
140 Brazil
148 Chile
154 Colombia
160 Ecuador
164 French Guiana
166 Guyana
170 Paraguay
174 Peru
180 Suriname
184 Uruguay
188 Venezuela

ARGENTINA

Total area	2,766,890 sq km	Population	33.1m
GDP	$200.3bn	GDP per head	$6,050
Capital	Buenos Aires	Other cities	Rosario, Cordoba

For years Argentina was called a first-world country with third-world management. This was the only logical explanation for its poor level of development. It suffered from high inflation and a lack of productive investment. There seemed to be little difference in the performance of the generals and the civilians who ruled the country. But under President Carlos Menem and his finance minister, Domingo Cavallo, Argentina made drastic free-market reforms. These are showing signs of leading the country down the road to sustained, non-inflationary growth.

History: nature's bounty

Successive governments have failed to exploit Argentina's natural riches as well as they could have. Nature has been generous: Argentina has a vast central region of prairies (*pampas*) where cattle are raised and wheat and soya are grown in abundance. The *pampas* are fed by rivers originating in the Andes. In the foothills, near Mendoza, grapes producing some excellent wines are grown. Further south, sheep are raised for wool and meat. Argentina makes some excellent cheeses in Chubut. Since Argentina is flat from Buenos Aires to the Andes, transport is easy. The country is criss-crossed by railways as well as by highways. From the north-west, much trade goes by the Paraguay river which, when it forms an estuary at Buenos Aires, becomes the River Plate. Buenos Aires, nearby La Plata and Bahia Blanca, further south, are the country's main harbours. The South Atlantic is full of fish, most notably abalone and krill, attracting pirate trawlers from around the world. There are no hurricanes. The worst that happens is an occasional drought and an outbreak of foot-and-mouth disease.

Man's mismanagement

Much of the country's history since independence from Spain has been dominated by strongman regimes. Argentina is a case of arrested development. At the turn of the century it was one of the richest countries in the world, attracting immigrants from Europe by the million as well as huge investments. But it became dominated by rich landowners belonging to the powerful Rural Society and their friends in the banks and stockmarket of Buenos Aires. This led to a populist reaction and to a long decline. President Hipolito

Yrigoyen (1916–22 and 1928–30) was the country's first popularly elected president. He was ousted in his second term by the armed forces in collusion with the friends of the Rural Society. The economy continued to grow, but mostly for the benefit of the better-off.

Peron was different

The inevitable reaction came in 1946. General Juan Domingo Peron, who had carefully cultivated the working classes while serving as minister of labour, won a free presidential election. He and his wife, Evita, gained the acclaim of the crowds. Unions became stronger. Government spending on social services grew. But so did inflation. Peron squandered the foreign-exchange reserves that Argentina had built up during the second world war by nationalising the railways and other public utilities. He promoted state intervention in industry (setting off a wave of inflation) and adopted some of the corporate-state ideas and political thuggery of Benito Mussolini. He became increasingly repressive towards his critics and the Catholic Church. Private investment slumped. Another reaction became inevitable.

Return of the generals

The army intervened in 1955, sending Peron into exile. But his hold on the masses was as strong as ever. A series of unstable military and civilian governments which held office from 1955 until 1972 found that whenever they tried to hold elections, Peronists won. Few were held; Peronist candidates were sometimes banned. Peron himself was finally allowed to return to the presidency in 1973. By that time, however, he was old and sick. He had become conservative in exile, to the dismay of a faction of young Peronists of the extreme left who decided to pursue their political struggle violently. Peron died in 1974 and was succeeded by his second wife, Isabelita, who had been vice-president. A former night-club dancer, Isabelita Peron had no political experience. She was open to the influence of her unscrupulous adviser, Jose Lopez Rega, who gained the reputation of being an Argentine Rasputin. Inflation surged; Argentina became more unstable than usual.

The dirty war

During Isabelita Peron's presidency (1974–76) Argentina descended into a hell of political extremism, sparked off by a wave of frightening extreme left-wing violence by the Marxist *Montoneros* and the People's Revolutionary Army. This provoked fears among the well-to-do and the army that the country was becoming ungovernable. First under Isabelita Peron and later under General Jorge Videla, who ousted her, the armed forces embarked on a brutal and ruthless campaign of extermination of suspected left-wing "subversives". They were mostly detained by men in civilian clothes, believed to be policemen and servicemen, and "disappeared". Perhaps 10,000 people were secretly killed, many of them after being tortured. General Videla, who became much hated and feared, was succeeded after an interregnum by General Leopoldo Galtieri, who quickly found himself in one of Argentina's usual economic crises in 1982.

Mrs Thatcher, Argentine democrat

The hard-drinking General Galtieri took a rash gamble: to distract public attention, he ordered the armed forces to seize the British Falkland Islands, which the Argentines had always claimed and called the *Islas Malvinas.* The operation took the British and the Americans by complete surprise and an Argentine governor was installed on the islands. In an even riskier gamble, however, the British prime minister, Margaret Thatcher, decided to take the islands back. British forces landed and defeated the Argentines in difficult conditions on rough terrain. The story might have been different if the Argentine air force's French-made *Exocet* missiles had exploded when hitting British warships. But many of them did not, and thousands of lives were saved.

Politics: a civilian takes over

Defeat forced General Galtieri from office and his successor paved the way for a presidential election which was won by Raul Alfonsin of the Radical Civic Union over an uninspiring Peronist candidate. This represented a turning point for Argentine democracy: Peronists could be defeated in free elections at last. During his stormy presidency (1983–89), Mr Alfonsin reasserted civilian control of the country and went a long way to restoring the rule of law. These were considerable achievements. Mr Alfonsin survived several coup attempts and he pushed through a controversial law which decreed that only the top leaders of the armed forces accused of ordering "disappearances" should be tried. This kept the armed forces relatively quiet.

Alfonsin's weaknesses

The economy remained heavily protected, with a large state sector. Mr Alfonsin failed to hold down government spending and thus inflation, which rose to 200% a month. Attempts to control prices collapsed. Mr Alfonsin was a man of the centre-left on economic policy. He was won over to the idea of privatisation but was never enthusiastic about it. He was no economist: his interests were politics and the law. Relations with the armed forces took up much of his time. He allowed the economy to slip out of control and suffered the humiliation of having to hand over power to his elected Peronist successor, Carlos Menem, five months ahead of schedule.

Menem the improbable

This pint-sized president with long sideburns, who came from a Lebanese family living in a remote province, turned Argentina upside down. At last the country enjoyed first-world management. In 1991, after two false starts with competent economy ministers who failed to stabilise the economy, Mr Menem gave the job to Domingo Cavallo, the brilliant head of a think-tank in Cordoba who could deliver a 45-minute speech on the Argentine economy in flawless English without any notes. Mr Menem and Mr Cavallo launched a wide-ranging privatisation campaign including the telephone, water and electricity services, the state oil company (YPF), the railways and the airline, bits of the military-industrial complex, television and railway stations, ports, shipping lines and even main highways. The peso was tied to the dollar. Inflation fell drastically to 8% in 1993. But this was not as low as American inflation and it raised concern that the peso would become over-valued.

A new outlook

Mr Menem followed his predecessor's policy towards the armed forces, slashing their budget while taking a conciliatory attitude to the generals themselves (he pardoned the worst civil-rights violators). He ended Argentina's long-standing and sterile hostility towards the United States by establishing a good working relationship with President Bush. He re-established relations with Britain and saw it as a free-trade ally in dealings with the GATT and the European Union. He tried to put the country on the world map by sending two frigates to the allied naval patrol during the war to recapture Kuwait from Iraq and a big UN peace-keeping unit to former Yugoslavia. Unlike Peron, the tub-thumping patriot, the Peronist Menem became an internationalist. He ratified the Tlatelolco treaty banning nuclear weapons from Latin America. His popularity grew. In December 1993 Mr Menem reached an agreement with

Mr Alfonsin's Radical Party under which the Radicals would support his bid to remove the 140-year-old ban on successive presidential terms so that he could stand for re-election when his mandate ended in July 1995. In return, Mr Menem agreed to shake up the Supreme Court and increase Radical Party representation.

Society: mixed up

The Argentines are a well-educated, predominantly European people. Their origins have led them at times to adopt a patronising attitude, some would call it arrogant, towards their fellow Latin Americans, especially those of American Indian or part-Indian origin. Their critics describe them, in an old joke, as "Italians who speak Spanish and think they are English". The national character is formed in part by the fact that the country is for the most part flat; a citizen of Buenos Aires has to drive for many hours to see a hill. This topographical factor may add to a sense of isolation and of being "at the end of the line". The Argentines know they are Europeans but live an ocean away from Europe. Buenos Aires is said to have one of the highest proportions of psychiatrists per head among the world's big cities.

In a sense Argentines were caught in a time warp for several decades. With little investment, businesses and industries stood still, few new writers of the stature of Jorge Luis Borges emerged and popular music continued to be dominated by the tango, a sensuous dance with often bitter or melancholic lyrics. However, it seemed only a matter of time, following the breath of fresh air of the Menem era, before the arts in Argentina – especially in books, films, television and theatre – would burst into life.

A great capital city

Buenos Aires, with its two airports, five underground railway lines, theatres, opera house, department stores, well-stocked bookshops and grand avenues, looks like a successful European city. Its people try to dress impeccably, and magazines follow French fashions closely. The wines are excellent. The steaks, *lomo* and *chorizo*, are among the world's best. Even in the poor districts, many of them on the outskirts, where slums have been created often by poor immigrants from Paraguay, the situation is not disastrous. Much remains to be done, however, to provide public housing, better health care and education.

The economy: Menem's strength

After campaigning as a populist, President Menem showed himself to be one of Argentina's most responsible and brave presidents. He adopted totally unPeronist policies. By 1993 he had privatised vast slabs of the state sector and was in a hurry to finish the job. He had slashed government expenditure and raised tax revenue, bringing the budget close to balance. He also joined a free-trade area with Brazil, Uruguay and Paraguay. This was, however, troubled by the strength of the peso; Brazilian exporters found they could undercut Argentine producers and Mr Cavallo was obliged to slap on some import surcharges. The economy minister claimed that the peso was still competitive. He pointed out that he had helped exporters by abolishing export taxes. A sweeping deregulation programme was launched. A pensions reform was designed to push fund managers into investing in the once-moribund stockmarket which, under Mr Cavallo, had roller-coastered upwards.

Unemployment worries

Massive privatisation had a negative political aspect: efficient private-sector companies which took over state concerns rightly purged large numbers of unneeded employees. YPF, for example, cut its workforce from 57,000 to 10,000 in 1993. Unemployment rose by 40% in the Buenos Aires area, and so did discontent. However, with GDP growing by 8.9% in 1991, 8.6% in 1992 and 6% in 1993, job creation could not be far off. The danger was that further growth could be inhibited by an over-valued peso. It was no accident that Argentina, traditionally a country with a healthy trade surplus, went into deficit in 1992 ($1.4 billion) and 1993 ($1.7 billion).

Rich again?

Nonetheless in the early 1990s Argentina looked in good shape. It had, however, looked in good shape at times in previous years and then collapsed. The Menem government had scored some impressive achievements. It was establishing an economic "track record" that could persuade more Argentines to put their money into savings that would be converted into productive investments, and to attract foreign investors interested in building factories rather than making a fast buck on the stockmarket. What was, at the turn of the century, one of the world's rich countries had an unmatched opportunity to become rich again.

Total area	2,766,890 sq km	% agricultural area	65
Capital	Buenos Aires	Highest point metres	Mount Aconcagua 6,960
Other cities	Rosario, Cordoba, La Plata, Mendoza	Main rivers	de la Plata, Paraguay, Parana, Colorado, Negro

The economy

GDP $bn	200.3	GDP per head $	6,050
% av. ann. growth in real GDP 1987–92	1.7	GDP per head in purchasing power parity (USA=100)	23.1

Origins of GDP	*% of total*	**Components of GDP**	*% of total*
Agriculture	6	Private consumption	85
Industry	31	Public consumption	...
of which:		Investment	17
manufacturing	22	Exports	7
Services	63	Imports	-8

Structure of manufacturing

			% of total
Agric. & food processing	20	Other	57
Textiles & clothing	10	Av. ann. increase in industrial output 1987–92	5.4
Machinery & transport	13		

Inflation and exchange rates

Consumer price 1993 av. ann. incr.	10.6%	Pesos per $ av. 1993	1.00
Av. ann. rate 1987–92	1,504%	Pesos per ecu av. 1993	1.12

Balance of payments, reserves, aid and debt

			$bn
Visible exports fob	12.2	Capital balance	8.6
Visible imports fob	-13.6	Overall balance	2.4
Trade balance	-1.4	Change in reserves	4.3
Invisible inflows	2.8	Level of reserves end Dec.	11.4
Invisible outflows	-9.8	Foreign debt	67.6
Net transfers	-0.03	as % of GDP	30.1
Current account balance	-8.4	Debt service	
as % of GDP	-4.2	as % of export earnings	34.9

Principal exports	*$bn fob*	**Principal imports**	*$bn cif*
Agricultural products	5.2	Machinery & industrial equip.	4.8
Oils & fats	1.1	Transport equipment	2.3
Cattle & meat	1.1	Chemicals	1.8
Minerals	0.8	Metals	1.1
Metals	0.8	Plastics	0.8

Main export destinations	*% of total*	**Main origins of imports**	*% of total*
USA	10.7	Brazil	22.7
Brazil	10.5	USA	20.3
Netherlands	10.4	Germany	7.5
Germany	6.1	Italy	5.1
Italy	4.7	Japan	4.6

Government

System Republic. Bicameral national congress, supreme court, and executive branch consisting of president, vice-president and cabinet.
Main political parties Justicialist Party, Radical Civil Union, Union of the Democratic Centre

Climate and topography

Mostly temperate climate; arid in southeast, subantarctic in southwest. Rich plains of pampas in northern half, flat to rolling plateau of Patagonia in south, Andes along western border.

People and society

Population m	33.1	% under 15	28.3
Pop. per sq km	12	% over 65	9.6
% urban	86	No. men per 100 women	98
% av. ann. growth 1987–92	1.2	Human Development Index	83.2
No. households m	7.4		

Life expectancy	*yrs*	**Education**	
Men	68	Spending as % of GDP	1.5
Women	75	Years of compulsory education	...
Crude birth rate	20	Adult literacy %	95
Crude death rate	9	Primary school enrolment %	100
Infant mortality		Secondary school enrolment %	74
per 1,000 live births	34	Tertiary education enrolment %	...

Workforce	*% of total*	**Consumer goods ownership**	
			Pop. per
Services	53		
Industry	34	Car	8.0
Agriculture	13	TV	4.5
% unemployed	7.0	Telephone	8.7

Ethnic groups	*% of total*	**Religious groups**	*% of total*
White	85	Roman Catholic	90
Mestizo, Indian and		Protestant	2
other non-white	15	Jewish	2

Tourism		**Health**	
Tourist arrivals m	2.7	Pop. per doctor	370
Tourist receipts $bn	0.9		

BOLIVIA

Total area	1,098,580 sq km	Population	7.8m
GDP	$5.1bn	GDP per head	$680
Capital	La Paz	Other cities	Santa Cruz, Cochabamba

Bolivia is a country of unusual extremes. Its capital, La Paz, is two miles high in the Andes and built on a steep slope. The rich live at the bottom of the slope; the poor live at the top. Bolivia's population is among the poorest in the world. Many people speak Aymara and Quechua (but can get along in Spanish). The rate of inflation, once 20,000% a year, was in 1993 less than 10%. Bolivia was the world's most unstable country, having suffered 190 coups since independence in 1825; in 1993 it looked tranquil. The free-market reforms of its state-smothered economy have been among the world's the most drastic. Bolivia is still desperately poor. But GDP growth in 1991, 1992 and 1993 was about 3% a year. With a new track record of political and economic stability, foreign investments were coming in.

History: revolutionary times

After independence from Spain, Bolivia offered the liberator, Simon Bolivar (for whom the country was named), the presidency for life. Bolivar accepted but did not take it seriously. Occasional wars have been disastrous. The War of the Pacific (1879–83) ended with Bolivia landlocked, having lost its outlet to the sea to Chile. In the 1930s Bolivia fought neighbouring Paraguay to a standstill over erroneously charted oilfields in the wastelands of the Chaco. Minerals have until recently dominated Bolivia. Under Spain, the silver mines at Potosi were a big money-spinner. Silver was followed by tin.

A social revolution

For decades until 1952 Bolivia was dominated by three powerful and rich tin-mining families, the Patinos, the Aramayos and the Hochschilds, and a group of powerful landowners. The tin-miners were extremely poor, always beholden to the company store for credit. Unexpectedly a sticks-and-stones social revolution carried Victor Paz Estenssoro to power in 1952, a year after he had been robbed of his victory in a presidential election by a military coup. Carried along by a wave of popular enthusiasm, he nationalised the tin mines and allowed the mass takeover of the big estates. Both became less efficient. Instead of working for a pittance on plantations called *latifundias*, many indigenous Indians were tilling their own small plots, called *minifundias*, which gave them an intangible prize: self-respect. For decades, Victor Paz, reserved and austere in and out of office, was the dominant political figure.

Instability was routine. Mr Paz (1952–56) was succeeded for four years by his vice-president, Hernan Siles Zuazo, and came back for a second term (1960–64). It was in 1964 that a military coup set off one of the most unstable periods in the country's history. It was led by General Rene Barrientos (1964–69), a handsome pilot and opportunist. It was during his presidency that a romantic but misguided attempt at rebellion led by the renowned Cuban-Argentine communist revolutionary, Dr Ernesto "Che" Guevara, failed and Guevara was shot. He had mistakenly chosen an area for his revolt where the peasants were proud smallholders and polite but unconvinced listeners to his Marxist ideas.

A brief return to civilian rule followed Barrientos's death in a plane crash. But in 1967–68 Bolivia was again ruled by a military man, this time General Alfredo Ovando Candia, a skilful temporiser (1969–70). After him came a radical leftist general, Juan Jose Torres, who was unmistakeably a *mestizo* (of mixed blood) unlike most Bolivian leaders who are of European extraction. After he was ousted, Torres was murdered in exile in Buenos Aires. He was replaced by a general of German extraction, Hugo Banzer (1971–78), who provided strongman rule without gross abuses of human rights and for the first time in many years gave the country a period of the stability that it desperately needed. Investments were made. Eventually General Banzer was persuaded to hold a presidential election. But it was rigged so blatantly in favour of his puppet that he was obliged to resign: the air force was threatening to bomb the presidential palace.

Dark days

Between July 1978 and July 1980 two further general elections were held, five presidents held office (none as a result of victory at the polls) and there were four coups, three of them successful. At the end of this chaotic period, General Luis Garcia Meza siezed power and Bolivia hit rock-bottom. Human rights were routinely violated and the short-lived regime was said to be closely linked to the drug trade. Subsequent sporadic elections were indecisive, often with Mr Paz and Mr Siles lacking clear majorities. Such elections were meant to be settled by Congress. But they created a political vacuum and gave ambitious generals the opportunity to intervene. Finally in 1982 the army handed over to Mr Siles, who had won most votes in the 1980 election.

The Siles shambles

Mr Siles's indecisive left-of-centre government was marked by strikes, three drastic cabinet changes, budget deficits and at one point 20,000%-a-year inflation. He was undermined by a man of the anti-communist left who should have been helping him: Juan Lechin, a radical who frequently presided over the Bolivian Labour Confederation (COB) when he was not in hiding. Mr Lechin saw his role as defending, with strikes and demonstrations, the rights of workers who were badly underpaid, come what may. IMF policies meant nothing to him. Mr Lechin's activities weakened Mr Siles, the man most likely to sympathise with the plight of the workers. The president went to the extreme of offering "co-government" to the COB. He was turned down. In 1985, after an indecisive election that as usual went to Congress for a decision, Mr Siles was succeeded by his old adversary, Victor Paz. Another revolution was about to begin.

Politics: a drastic reform

At the start of his final presidency in 1985, Victor Paz was ruthless. He told his able finance minister, Juan Cariaga, to pay out, on a daily basis, only the revenue that he had received on the previous day. State enterprises were told to balance their books and had their subsidies cut off. Many uneconomic tin mines closed. The wages of state employees were frozen. Foreign exchange was sold at auctions that set the rate. It was drastic and, with the crucial support in Congress of Hugo Banzer, now a civilian politician, it worked. Within weeks, inflation fell to 10% and often less. Victor Paz's leftish successor, Jaime Paz Zamora, continued his reformist policies, again with the firm backing of Mr Banzer. Jaime Paz handed the country to his constitutionally elected successor, the conservative Gonzalo Sanchez de Lozada (who had been Victor Paz's economy minister). Incredibly, Bolivia had freely elected three consecutive civilian presidents and was carrying out non-inflationary export-oriented free-market policies with considerable success.

Society: two worlds

There are at least two worlds in Bolivia. One is modern, where business is discharged as efficiently as anywhere in Latin America. The other is the world of the poor peasants who farm tiny plots of land or survive as street vendors. To dull the pangs of hunger, poor people chew coca leaves.

These two worlds scarcely meet. If Bolivia's economy continues its stable growth, however, expectations among the country's poor will rise. They have already shown signs of listening to the extravagant promises of populists.

The economy: a long way to go

Bolivia's future lies in keeping government small and hoping that investors will create more jobs in a stable business environment. There are unexploited deposits of gold, sulphur and semi-precious minerals in the hills. Bolivia is self-sufficient in oil and natural gas and has been exporting gas to Argentina. A pipeline to Brazil is to be built. The once-empty lowlands around Santa Cruz are producing wheat. There is a danger that the country will be split into a relatively prosperous lowland, centred on Santa Cruz, and a dirt-poor *altiplano*, the arid, near-barren highlands centred on La Paz, part of which looks like a moonscape, where hundreds of thousands of peasants scratch a pathetic living. In La Paz itself, filled with women wearing ethnic dresses and brown bowler hats, usually suckling a baby and trying to sell a trayful of vegetables or anything from batteries and toothbrushes to socks, the underground economy is clearly bigger than the official one. It will take a tremendous effort and large investments to raise wage levels and improve the lot of Bolivia's poor.

Omnipresent drugs

The drug trade, from coca-growing farmers to the producers of cocaine, could become so powerful that the government succumbs to its money and the killers it can hire. There have been some unmistakeable signs that this process is under way but that it is by no means irreversible. The government consistently fails to achieve the goals of destruction of coca-growing areas agreed with the aid-giving United States.

Another worry is that Bolivians may become increasingly restless about the slow speed of the trickle-down process of economic growth. Many Bolivians feel that, regardless of the economic reforms, they are just as poor as ever. This has encouraged Mr Sanchez de Lozada to try to neutralise Bolivia's populists. He has given cabinet posts to some of them. He has also launched a novel privatisation scheme under which the purchaser of a state enterprise would buy 50% of the shares and the remainder would be distributed to the population in the form of contributions to private-sector pension funds.

Total area	1,098,580 sq km	% agricultural area	28
Capital	La Paz[a]	Highest point metres	Nevado Illampu 6,400
Other cities	Santa Cruz, Cochabamba	Main rivers	Beri, Honomas, Paragua

The economy

GDP $bn	5.1	GDP per head $	680
% av. ann. growth in real GDP 1987–92	3.6	GDP per head in purchasing power parity (USA=100)	9.8

Origins of GDP	*% of total*	**Components of GDP**	*% of total*
Agriculture	29	Private consumption	77
Industry	37	Public consumption	15
of which:		Investment	14
manufacturing	...	Exports	18
Services	34	Imports	-23

Structure of manufacturing

			% of total
Agric. & food processing	37	Other	53
Textiles & clothing	8	Av. ann. increase in industrial	
Machinery & transport	1	output 1987–92	2.4

Inflation and exchange rates

Consumer price 1993 av. ann. incr.	8.5%	Bolivianos per $ av. 1993	4.48
Av. ann. rate 1987–93	14.7%	Bolivianos per ecu av. 1993	5.02

Balance of payments, reserves, aid and debt

			$bn
Visible exports fob	0.6	Capital balance	0.3
Visible imports fob	-1.0	Overall balance	-0.1
Trade balance	-0.4	Change in reserves	-0.1
Invisible inflows	0.2	Level of reserves end Dec.	0.2
Invisible outflows	-0.5	Foreign debt	4.2
Net transfers	0.02	as % of GDP	83.6
Current account balance	-0.5	Debt service	
as % of GDP	-8.3	as % of export earnings	39.1

Principal exports	*$bn fob*	**Principal imports**	*$bn cif*
Natural gas	0.2	Raw materials &	
Zinc	0.1	semi-manufactures	0.6
Tin	0.1	Capital goods	0.4
Gold	0.07	Consumer goods	0.2

Main export destinations	*% of total*	**Main origins of imports**	*% of total*
Argentina	21.5	USA	23.3
UK	18.1	Brazil	14.5
USA	16.0	Japan	12.6
Belgium-Luxembourg	11.7	Argentina	10.4

Government

System Republic, with president elected for 4-year term. Bicameral National Congress consists of Chamber of Senators and Chamber of Deputies.
Main political parties Nationalist Revolutionary Movement, Movement of the Revolutionary Left, Nationalist Democratic Action

Climate and topography

Variable climate, depending on altitude. Humid and tropical to cold and semi-arid. Rugged Andes Mountains with a highland plateau, and hills. Also lowland Amazon basin.

People and society

Population m	7.8	% under 15	42.5
Pop. per sq km	7	% over 65	3.4
% urban	51	No. men per 100 women	97
% av. ann. growth 1987–92	2.9	Human Development Index	39.8
No. households m	...		

Life expectancy	*yrs*	**Education**	
Men	59	Spending as % of GDP	2.4
Women	64	Years of compulsory education	8
Crude birth rate	33	Adult literacy %	78
Crude death rate	9	Primary school enrolment %	79
Infant mortality		Secondary school enrolment %	34
per 1,000 live births	82	Tertiary education enrolment %	23

Workforce	*% of total*	**Consumer goods ownership**	
			Pop. per
Services	34		
Industry	19	Car	200.0
Agriculture	47	TV	...
% unemployed	5.8	Telephone	34.5

Ethnic groups	*% of total*	**Religious groups**	*% of total*
Quechua	30	Roman Catholic	95
Aymara	25		
Mixed	25–30		
European	5–15		

Tourism		**Health**	
Tourist arrivals m	0.2	Pop. per doctor	1,530
Tourist receipts $bn	0.1		

a Seat of government, Suore legal capital.

BRAZIL

Total area	8,511,965 sq km	Population	156.8m
GDP	$424bn	GDP per head	$2,780
Capital	Brasilia	Other cities	Sao Paulo, Rio de Janeiro

Brazil has called itself the "land of the future" so often that one of its many military presidents coined a new slogan. He proclaimed that "the future has already arrived!" He was exaggerating. True, Brazil has an astonishingly dynamic economy. But its politicians have proved in the main to be incompetent and occasionally crooked muddlers whose attention to the needs of the poor masses has been insignificant. Nonetheless, if Brazil's rapidly expanding economic resources could be distributed more fairly, a vast domestic market might be created; Brazil might even become an engine of international economic growth.

History: unchanging ways

A Portuguese mariner, Pedro Alvares Cabral, bumped into Brazil in 1500 while on his way (he thought) to India. Subsequent expeditions revealed a huge new continent which the Portuguese began to develop. Sugar plantations were started with American Indian slave labour. There were clashes between slave-owners who wanted their acquisitions to work and the Jesuit missionaries who wanted them to convert to Christianity. The Indians were decimated by disease and the survivors, scared of slavery, fled to the interior. So the Portuguese turned to another source of slaves: Africa. The trade peaked in the second half of the 17th century with about 8,000 slaves shipped from Africa every year.

Big and disorganised

Some white hunters of Indian slaves, known as *bandeirantes*, turned to prospecting and discovered gold in the interior. They created ever-expanding borders for Brazil. Their successors today are carving out land in the Amazon jungle, cutting down the forest and prospecting for gold. Government was a loose affair, with Lisbon assuming that Brazil was an extension of Portugal but not doing much about it. Locally, power was delegated mostly to communities; health and education was in the hands of the Catholic Church. A new elite comprising powerful landowners, called "colonels", with close ties to traders at nearby ports, evolved.

"Coffee with milk"

Independence came painlessly in 1889 and the country

turned into a federation: individual states could raise taxes, obtain foreign loans and even impose import tariffs. This arrangement suited the "colonels" and their friends. Two states became powerful: coffee-growing Sao Paulo and cattle-raising Minas Gerais. They set up what was called the coffee-with-milk alliance. To a certain extent this powerful link persists today.

The "New State" of Getulio Vargas

Turmoil caused by the Wall Street crash in 1929 led to a military coup which installed a civilian politician from the southern state of Rio Grande do Sul, Getulio Vargas, as president in 1930. Vargas ruled Brazil for two periods totalling 19 years. He became a strongman, applying more central control and diminishing the coffee-with-milk alliance. In 1937 he assumed dictatorial powers and established a nationalist, corporate state somewhat along the lines of Italy's. It included a strong emphasis on industrialisation partly financed by foreign debts and partly by printing money, leading to high inflation.

Brazil looks inward

Vargas was succeeded in 1956 by one of Brazil's most popular post-war figures, Juscelino Kubitschek, a strong democrat who created a controversial new capital, Brasilia, in the interior of the country. It contains some fine examples of modern Brazilian architecture. In the short term Brasilia added to the country's indebtedness; in the long term its grandiose vision opened to development the neglected, sparsely populated and often uncultivated plains of the interior. Brazilians looked back on the Kubitschek era with *saudade* (nostalgic longing) after the army seized power in 1964 from President Joao Goulart, a populist radical. Goulart had allowed inflation to increase and the country to become almost insolvent, and was challenging the influence of the armed forces. General Humberto Castello Branco, a distinguished military intellectual who had served in the Brazilian expeditionary force in Italy during the second world war, was installed as president.

The long night of the generals

Castello Branco's finance minister, Roberto Campos, brought inflation under control through a temporary recession, created a stockmarket and a central bank and headed the country in the direction of stable, export-led growth. At the same time, however, Castello Branco banned all political parties and barred many politicians from public life for ten years by so-called Institutional Acts. Suspected communists or other "subversives" were interrogated and tortured by military units and the security police around the country. Some of the radicals served in the guerrilla group led by the Marxist Carlos Marighela, who kidnapped and released an American ambassador (unharmed) and hijacked several airliners to Cuba. Others who suffered torture included non-violent radicals, trade unionists and left-wing intellectuals. A succession of military presidents, often elected at the end of private presidential campaigns among the officer corps, succeeded Castello Branco. They could take credit for Brazil's "economic miracle", the basis of which had been laid by Vargas and Campos.

Miraculous for some

Industrialisation, mainly in the Sao Paulo area but also in many other cities, came at a price: high inflation, frequently running for month after month at an annual rate of about 200%. The gap between rich and poor grew: in 1960 it was reckoned that the richest 10% of the population received 40% of the national income; by 1980 they received 51%. Unable to set the country on a non-inflationary course, and increasingly unpopular, the generals decided to withdraw, in good order, to their barracks. They did so, after a period of "democratic opening" and let Brazil's bumbling civilian politicians take office again.

Politics: when freedom fails

The first presidential election, in 1985, involved only members of Congress. Tancredo Neves, a 74-year-old veteran democratic politician, won, but died before his inauguration. His vice-president, Jose Sarney, who took his place, proved to be a mediocrity incapable of dealing with inflation and the foreign debt or to find uncultivated land to give to the country's 10m landless peasants. Congress, split into factions, was no help. The biggest opposition party under the generals, the Brazilian Democratic Movement, had no ideological line: its members included ardent capitalists and ex-Marxists. Congress wrote an impractical new constitution which even set limits on interest rates.

Impeachment crisis

Mr Sarney was succeeded in 1989 by the handsome, dynamic governor of the tiny north-eastern state of Alagoas, Fernando Collor de Mello, who defeated a left-wing unionist and leader of the Workers' Party, Luis Inacio ("Lula") da

Silva with 53% of the vote. Mr Collor was aided as finance minister by the able, attractive but confrontational Zelia Cardoso de Mello (no relation). Their ambitious "Collor Plan" to halt inflation failed, like its predecessors. Zelia Cardoso, out of favour with international banks and the Brazilian business class, lost her job. So, after a dramatic impeachment debate in Congress, did President Collor in December 1992. He had been accused by his disaffected brother and in Congress of complicity with his 1989 election campaign manager, Paulo Cesar Farias, in a number of corrupt practices including misappropriation of public funds.

A political failure

Brazilian democracy worked in that Mr Collor was succeeded by his number two and not by a power-hungry general. But the new president, Itamar Franco, was a wilful mediocrity like Mr Sarney, who found it hard to keep his ministers. By the end of 1993 he had let inflation reach 30% a month. A new scandal involving parliamentarians and public-works contracts in 1993 appeared likely to undermine the reputation of civilian politicians even more. Ominously, the air force commander had complained that the armed forces were "asphyxiated" by a cash shortage and suffering from "systematic demoralisation". It was worrying as well as reassuring that the generals began to make statements that they had no intention of re-taking power.

Society: weak on culture

In the colonial period, Jesuits ran colleges and seminaries but there was no university; bright sons of wealthy families had to study in Portugal. Books were imported since there was no printing press. Today Brazilian universities do not enjoy a high international reputation, and bookshops are hard to find in some cities. State-run secondary education is also poor. The fear is that an unemployable under-class is being created.

Multi-racial peace so far

Brazil is a multi-racial society run by whites and made up also of people of mixed blood, blacks and Indians. South of Sao Paulo, Brazil looks like part of well-to-do rural Western Europe. Sao Paulo looks like a modern, dynamic, multi-racial American city replete with skyscrapers. Rio is a melting-pot. Further up the east coast in Salvador (Bahia), blacks predominate on the streets while in Belem, on the north coast, many of the faces are Indian. In or near many cities are poor districts, where families start by building a one-room home and add more rooms when they can afford to do so. Then there are the slums (*favelas*): some are well-managed with electricity and running water; others are fetid and filthy and a disgrace to Brazil. Poverty in Rio, where 20% of the population lives in *favelas*, has led to an almost uncontrollable crime wave. Slum gangs sporadically terrorise sunbathers on Rio's Copacabana and Ipanema beaches. The fear is that this will lead to more serious social unrest.

Soft on the environment

The murder in 1988 of Chico Mendes, chief of the rubber-tappers' union and a prominent ecologist, drew international attention to Brazil's neglect of its environment and especially the uncontrolled cutting of timber in Amazonia. A United Nations conference on the environment was held with some success in Rio de Janeiro in 1992. The government made an effort to control the destruction of the jungle and the invasion by settlers of lands occupied by primitive Indian peoples. But it seemed to lack the means, and the political will, to act decisively.

The economy: think big and export

Brazil evolved slowly as a collection of port cities with special interests inland. Since Lisbon could not provide colonial Brazil with goods that Brazilians needed, the settlers had to export to obtain foreign exchange for their purchases. From the start Brazil was export-oriented. By the late 19th century the Brazilian economy was dominated by coffee, which was exported all over the world. Sao Paulo, and the nearby port of Santos, was its heart. By the 1970s Brazil was an industrial giant. Sao Paulo was still the heart, but many other cities, including Belo Horizonte, Porto Alegre and Fortaleza, were growing dramatically. Brazilians thought big. For example, the Companhia Vale do Rio Doce built a railway hundreds of miles into the interior to bring iron ore to a coastal terminal and profited from the investment to bring grains on the same line to an adjacent grain terminal. Costs were much lower than those in North America.

Productive investments

At one point a Brazilian company, Engesa, was the world's biggest exporter of armoured cars. Another company was selling small airliners to the world market. A third boasted it had sold a complete new foundry to an American steel-maker. A fourth was building roads in the Middle East.

Many sold orange juice to Florida. Huge dams, most notably Itaipu, harnessed the country's rivers. Wheat and soya-bean harvests increased sharply as new lands in the interior were brought under cultivation. To pay for much of this, Brazil contracted huge foreign loans. What distinguished the Brazilians from some other South American borrowers was that they usually spent the money on bricks-and-mortar productive investments rather than imports of consumer goods. It was not a complete success, however. One of the military rulers, General Joao Figueiredo, joked bitterly that the production cost of the output of one steel plant was equivalent to its weight in gold.

Needed: computers and calculators

One of Mr Collor's achievements was to open up the economy by cutting import tariffs, launching a privatisation programme and by promoting a free-trade area with Argentina, Uruguay and Paraguay. The old system of protected, state-led economic development was being abandoned; entrepreneurs were being left to survive in an open market. The economy could grow during a period of high inflation thanks to a sophisticated system of indexation of wages and prices which provided a crazy sort of stability for those with computers and calculators. The trouble was that the poor had neither. Inflation has defied various attempts to reduce it, including the "Collor Plan", under which personal and corporate savings were sequestered in order to halt inflation in its tracks while the public sector was cut. Eventually the money was released. Another anti-inflation plan was launched in 1994. It has proved easier to bring central-government spending under control than to impose discipline on spendthrift state governors. Nonetheless, in 1993 Brazil's GDP grew by about 4.5%, it recorded a trade surplus in June 1994 of about $38 billion and it had foreign-exchange reserves of some $15 billion.

Brazil was dogged by poor international economic relations. Its foreign debt has been rescheduled, giving it more time to pay, but it has slipped into arrears on interest payments and amortisation even though it has a substantial trade surplus and foreign-exchange reserves. Promises contained in frequent "letters of intent" to the International Monetary Fund, of good economic behaviour in return for requested loans, were not kept. Relations with creditor banks and creditor governments were also patchy. Nonetheless, for all its faults, Brazil remains the most dynamic country in Latin America and the "land of the future".

Total area	8,511,965 sq km	% agricultural area	27
Capital	Brasilia	Highest point metres	Pico da Neblina 3,014
Other cities	Sao Paulo, Rio de Janeiro, Belo Horizonte	Main rivers	Amazon, Parana, Quarai

The economy

GDP $bn	424	GDP per head $	2,776
% av. ann. growth in real GDP 1987–92	-0.1	GDP per head in purchasing power parity (USA=100)	23.7

Origins of GDP	*% of total*	**Components of GDP**	*% of total*
Agriculture	11	Private consumption	65
Industry	34	Public consumption	14
of which:		Investment	19
manufacturing	25	Exports	8.5
Services	55	Imports	-5

Structure of manufacturing

			% of total
Agric. & food processing	13	Other	52
Textiles & clothing	12	Av. ann. increase in industrial	
Machinery & transport	23	output 1987–92	...

Inflation and exchange rates

Consumer price 1993 av. ann. incr.	2,146%	Cruzeiros per $ av. 1993	326.1
Av. ann. rate 1987–93	736%	Cruzeiros per ecu av. 1993	365.2

Balance of payments, reserves, aid and debt

			$bn
Visible exports fob	36.1	Capital balance	12.6
Visible imports fob	-20.6	Overall balance	17.7
Trade balance	15.5	Change in reserves	15.0
Invisible inflows	5.0	Level of reserves end Dec.	13.6
Invisible outflows	-16.3	Foreign debt	121.1
Net transfers	2.1	as % of GDP	31.3
Current account balance	6.3	Debt service	
as % of GDP	1.5	as % of export earnings	31.3

Principal exports	*$bn fob*	**Principal imports**	*$bn cif*
Metal products	6.1	Raw materials	7.2
Transport equipment	4.2	Capital goods	6.3
Soya products	2.7	Oil & products	4.1
Ores	2.5		

Main export destinations	*% of total*	**Main origins of imports**	*% of total*
EU	29.6	USA	24.2
Central & South America	20.8	EU	22.3
Asia	15.5	Aladi	17.5
USA	10.6	Middle East	13.8

Government

System Federal republic. 26 states and one federal district. President elected for 5-year term. Bicameral National Congress with 91-member Senate and 503-member Chamber of Deputies.
Main political parties Workers' Party, Brazilian Democratic Movement Party, Liberal Front Party, Brazilian Social Democracy Party

Climate and topography

Predominantly tropical but variable depending on distance from sea and altitude. Mostly flat with rolling lowlands in north. Some plains, hills, mountains and narrow coastal belt in south.

People and society

Population m	156.8	% under 15	35.4
Pop. per sq km	19	% over 65	4.4
% urban	75	No. men per 100 women	99
% av. ann. growth 1987–92	2.0	Human Development Index	73.0
No. households m	33.4		

Life expectancy	*yrs*	**Education**	
Men	64	Spending as % of GDP	3.9
Women	69	Years of compulsory education	6
Crude birth rate	23	Adult literacy %	81
Crude death rate	7	Primary school enrolment %	88
Infant mortality		Secondary school enrolment %	39
per 1,000 live births	67	Tertiary education enrolment %	12

Workforce	*% of total*	**Consumer goods ownership**	
Services	47		*Pop. per*
Industry	25	Car	9.6
Agriculture	28	TV	4.7
% unemployed	5.9	Telephone	10.4

Ethnic groups	*% of total*	**Religious groups**	*% of total*
White	55	Roman Catholic	90
Mixed	38		
Black	6		

Tourism		**Health**	
Tourist arrivals m	1.1	Pop. per doctor	1,080
Tourist receipts $bn	1.4		

CHILE

Total area	756,945 sq km	Population	13.6m
GDP	$37.1bn	GDP per head	$2,730
Capital	Santiago	Other cities	Vina del Mar

The long dictatorship of General Augusto Pinochet was an aberration in Chile's history, as was the Marxist government of Salvador Allende which the general ended in a bloody coup in 1973. Chile has a long and distinguished democratic tradition, to which it reverted after General Pinochet stepped down in 1989. The general left a record for political brutality unmatched in contemporary Latin America apart from Guatemala, Haiti and Cuba. He also bequeathed to his civilian successors the best-run economy of the region.

History: an exceptional record

The constitution of 1833, approved 15 years after Chile's independence from Spain, lasted until 1925. Under it a multi-party system flourished, there were regular peaceful transfers of power after elections and the army played little part in politics. The economy was based on the export of wheat, copper, nitrates and silver, and was heavily influenced by mining companies, banks and big landowners. Trade unions and the Communist Party were formed. In 1920, however, a strong sense of social injustice led to the election of a populist, Arturo Alessandri, in 1920, and to a period of instability. Alessandri proved an ineffectual reformer and was ousted by discontented and unpaid army officers in 1924. He returned after a second coup but was ousted again, this time by the defence minister, Colonel Carlos Ibanez. The colonel assumed dictatorial powers but fell in 1931 and was succeeded by several brief governments including one with communist ministers.

Politics: Frei showed the way

The first coherent attempt at reform was made by Eduardo Frei (1964–70), a Christian Democrat who introduced cautious but substantial land-reforms, built public housing and improved health and education. He presided over a remarkably open society at a time when other Latin American countries were ruled by dictators. His philosophy had a seminal influence on social democrats throughout the region. However, Frei's open society encouraged extremists. One group said his land reforms were slow and small, and it grabbed land. There was a palpable shift to the left in Chilean society.

In the 1970 election, the Christian Democrats made a disastrous error: instead of picking a man of moderation who would follow Frei's careful reformist path, they chose Radomiro Tomic, a left-wing opportunist whose platform rivalled that of the Marxist Salvador Allende (at the head of a Socialist-Communist electoral alliance). Centrist voters abandoned the Christian Democrats, who came third (27.8%) after Allende (36.3%) and the conservative Jorge Alessandri (35%). Since no candidate had a clear majority, the final decision was up to Congress. Its anti-Marxist majority could have voted Alessandri into office. Instead it chose to respect the winner of a plurality and, after obtaining promises from Allende that he would behave like a good democrat, elected him.

The Marxist takes over

The new president began to seize land and take over the private sector. By controlling prices and increasing wages drastically, he forced companies into insolvency. Then he sent in government "interveners". Inflation rose to 500%. The government was accumulating power, befriending Cuba's President Castro and becoming increasingly Marxist. There were, however, no political prisons, no mass murders and no torture chambers. Allende may have been rash and extreme but he was also a civilised physician.

The rightists respond

In 1973 General Pinochet seized power and Allende died in the presidential palace, a probable suicide. Thousands fled the country. Many were killed in a widespread "anti-communist" purge. Torture chambers were established by the secret police. A reign of terror existed for anybody with a reputation for being a leftist. This was Chile's darkest moment. However, General Pinochet was not alone: he enjoyed support among the middle and upper classes on the ground that he was better than "communist chaos". Was the coup orchestrated from the United States? Available evidence suggests that, while the Americans were pleased to see Allende go, and had examined ways of getting rid of him, the support which mattered came from Brazil. General Pinochet followed closely the Brazilian generals' approach in seizing power in 1964 from a leftist president.

The hard line

Chile was ruled by decree by General Pinochet as the head of a junta with the chiefs of the navy, the air force and the paramilitary police (*carabineros*). But the general was top dog. Chile endured repressive military rule. Slowly it was lifted then, if the opposition seemed likely to get out of hand, re-imposed again. As the regime felt more confident, it allowed criticism (although some independent-minded journalists were beaten up).

The centre prevails

General Pinochet called a referendum in 1988 which asked the country to approve his remaining in office. He lost by 55% to 48%. This was followed by a presidential and general election in 1989 in which he was represented as presidential candidate by his brilliant and eccentric finance minister, Hernan Buchi. The Christian Democratic candidate, Patricio Aylwin, a lawyer-politician in the Frei tradition who had assembled a wide electoral alliance, beat Mr Buchi by 55% to 29%. Mr Aylwin was succeeded, after a presidential election in 1993, by Frei's son, Eduardo, at the head of a Christian Democrat-led alliance, with 58% of the vote, followed by Arturo Alessandri, a conservative, with 24%. Chile was back on its democratic track again, heading, it seemed, towards prosperity. Its dark era was over.

Troops on the streets

However, General Pinochet stayed on as army commander, determined to prevent any investigation of civil-rights abuses under his regime (in 1978 he had declared an amnesty for such crimes). When it was suggested that servicemen might testify in court about what had happened to the "disappeared", the general ordered troops in full combat gear on to the streets for an "exercise". Mr Aylwin promptly suggested servicemen might testify in secret but was criticised by his own side and withdrew the proposal.

Society: looking up

Chileans, who are mostly of European stock, are well-educated, articulate and notable for a lack of *machismo*. The Aylwin government concentrated on alleviating the poverty in which some 4m Chileans live, using money obtained from tax increases.

The economy: free-market downs and ups

General Pinochet began his presidency with a cut in government spending that brought inflation crashing down in two years. He then introduced reforms to reduce the power of the state. Many state enterprises were returned to their owners or privatised. The budget deficit was slashed. The economy slowly came back to life. Then in 1982 it collapsed: the peso was over-valued and the local capital market virtually uncontrolled; millions had been borrowed from foreign banks to build offices and homes that nobody could afford. The government had to take back companies it had privatised. GDP fell by 8%. It looked like a slump.

Buchi's success

Starting in 1984, Mr Buchi applied the same free-market policies. But he kept a competitive exchange rate and controls on the capital market. Inflation was subdued. Exports began to boom. Foreign investors were attracted by the privatisations. The state got out of the old-age pension business and left it to private funds, which were told to invest in the stockmarket (which they did, giving it a new impetus). Foreign debt was reduced drastically by allowing debt paper to be used to buy state enterprises that were being sold off.

Carry on, please

Mr Aylwin and his able finance minister, Alejandro Foxley, followed Mr Buchi's policies with a stronger emphasis on public health and education. The 1993 budget increased social spending by $6 billion. The government continued to encourage foreign investment ($6 billion came in from 1985 to 1992). GDP, which had grown at an average of 5.7% a year since the mid-1980s, shot up by 10% in 1992 and (to avoid over-heating) a "modest" 6% in 1993. Privatisation, which brought the number of state enterprises down from about 500 to some 50, was likely to continue. Negotiations were planned on a free-trade pact with the United States.

Non-traditional

Chile used to be synonymous with copper. Now it is equally well-known for its exports of apples, fine wines, salmon (40,000 tons in 1992), fishmeal, cellulose, cement and footwear. Inflation was running at about 12% in 1993. The trade surplus, however, slipped from $1.5 billion in 1991 to a deficit of $900m in 1993. Exports were hurt by the world economic slowdown; imports were encouraged by low tariffs averaging 10%. Nonetheless, foreign-exchange reserves excluding gold were running steadily at almost $10 billion in 1993 so there was no concern. Chile became a model, for other reform-minded Latin American governments, of sustained, non-inflationary, export-led growth.

Total area	756,945 sq km	% agricultural area	23
Capital	Santiago	Highest point metres	Ojos de Salado 6,880
Other cities	Vina del Mar, Valparaiso, Talcahuano, Concepcion		

The economy

GDP $bn	37.1	GDP per head $	2,730
% av. ann. growth in real GDP 1987–92	7.3	GDP per head in purchasing power parity (USA=100)	31.9

Origins of GDP	*% of total*	**Components of GDP**	*% of total*
Agriculture	9	Private consumption	66
Industry	36	Public consumption	9
of which:		Investment	23
manufacturing	21	Exports	34
Services	55	Imports	-31

Structure of manufacturing

			% of total
Agric. & food processing	24	Other	64
Textiles & clothing	7	Av. ann. increase in industrial	
Machinery & transport	5	output 1987–92	7.1

Inflation and exchange rates

Consumer price 1993 av. ann. incr.	12.6%	Pesos per $ av. 1993	431.0
Av. ann. rate 1987–93	18.5%	Pesos per ecu av. 1993	482.8

Balance of payments, reserves, aid and debt

			$bn
Visible exports fob	10.0	Capital balance	2.9
Visible imports fob	-9.2	Overall balance	2.5
Trade balance	0.8	Change in reserves	1.9
Invisible inflows	3.0	Level of reserves end Dec.	9.7
Invisible outflows	-4.7	Foreign debt	19.4
Net transfers	0.4	as % of GDP	49.3
Current account balance	-0.6	Debt service	
as % of GDP	-1.6	as % of export earnings	20.9

Principal exports	*$bn fob*	**Principal imports**	*$bn cif*
Industrial products	4.0	Intermediate goods	5.4
Copper	3.9	Capital goods	2.8
Food & fish products	1.2	Consumer goods	1.9

Main export destinations	*% of total*	**Main origins of imports**	*% of total*
Japan	16.7	USA	20.0
USA	16.1	Brazil	10.2
Germany	5.8	Japan	10.1
UK	5.8	Argentina	6.6
Taiwan	5.0	Germany	6.5
South Korea	4.6	Nigeria	3.3
Brazil	4.4	France	2.9

Government

System Republic with elected president and bicameral National Congress. 13 administrative regions divided into 51 regions. All local officials are appointed by the president.

Main political parties Christian Democratic Party, Socialist Party, National Renovation Party

Climate and topography

Temperate climate; desert in north, cool and damp in south. Low coastal mountains with fertile central valley. Rugged Andes in the east.

People and society

Population m	13.6	% under 15	30.4
Pop. per sq km	19	% over 65	6.4
% urban	86	No. men per 100 women	98
% av. ann. growth 1987–92	1.6	Human Development Index	86.4
No. households m	3.0		

Life expectancy	*yrs*	**Education**	
Men	69	Spending as % of GDP	2.9
Women	76	Years of compulsory education	8
Crude birth rate	22	Adult literacy %	93
Crude death rate	6	Primary school enrolment %	86
Infant mortality		Secondary school enrolment %	74
per 1,000 live births	17	Tertiary education enrolment %	18

Workforce	*% of total*	**Consumer goods ownership**	
Services	52		*Pop. per*
Industry	30	Car	20.4
Agriculture	18	TV	4.9
% unemployed	5.0	Telephone	14.7

Ethnic groups	*% of total*	**Religious groups**	*% of total*
European	95	Roman Catholic	89
Indian	3	Protestant	11

Tourism		**Health**	
Tourist arrivals m	1.0	Pop. per doctor	1,160
Tourist receipts $bn	0.5		

COLOMBIA

Total area	1,138,914 sq km	Population	33.4m
GDP	$44.6bn	GDP per head	$1,330
Capital	Bogota	Other cities	Medellin, Cali, Barranquilla

Colombia is one of the world's most violent countries. It is, however, slowly evolving into a more open democracy with good prospects for higher economic growth. If the country's remaining guerrillas could be absorbed into civil society, and if its remaining drug barons could be eliminated, Colombia could prosper. But those are two big ifs.

History: a tendency to fight

Under the Spanish, New Granada with its capital at Bogota and its main slave port at Cartagena was an important colonial outpost and gold producer. The American Indian population, skilled at making gold ornaments, was not killed off or repressed; many Indians were assimilated through intermarriage. Colombia became independent in 1820 with the collapse of the dream of the liberator, Simon Bolivar, of a Greater Colombia embracing Venezuela, Ecuador and Bolivia. Geography has affected Colombia's history: it is a large, mountainous country with poor communications, encouraging the development of local bosses and rivalries. Outbreaks of fighting erupted sporadically throughout the 19th century, often pitting anti-clerical Liberals against pro-Church Conservatives. The depths were reached in the "war of 1,000 days" between 1899 and 1903 in which some 100,000 people were killed.

Brutal times

The next outbreak came in 1948 after the two parties became more extreme, the Conservatives veering towards fascism and the Liberals towards left-wing populism. The leftist leader, Jorge Eliecer Gaitan, was assassinated. Riots erupted in Bogota and the dark period known as The Violence began. It lasted, in distant parts, until the 1960s and took an estimated 200,000–300,000 lives. The Violence was rooted in the chronic lawlessness of the country, especially its remoter areas, and accentuated it. In 1957 the Liberals and Conservatives agreed on a power-sharing pact that stopped much but not all of the killing. The presidency was to go alternately to a Liberal and a Conservative. Seats in cabinet and Congress were to be split equally between the two parties. This plainly undemocratic deal profited the powerful landed gentry and business interests who formed the elite. But it stopped much of The Violence. A distinguished Colombian, Alberto Lleras Camargo, became president in 1958 under the terms of the accord, which were kept by both sides.

The rise of the outlaws

At this point lawlessness took two new directions: Marxist rebellion and drug-trafficking. Half a dozen rebel bands mounted a violent challenge to the power of the oligarchy. One was led by a priest, Camilo Torres, who was subsequently killed. Another, one of the biggest, was the Colombian Revolutionary Armed Forces (FARC), led by Manuel ("Sure Shot") Marulanda. One group's speciality was blowing up the pipeline taking oil from wells in the interior to a coastal terminal. Many guerrilla gangs kidnapped people from wealthy families and ransomed them for large sums. Some were said to have taken on a new and well-paid job: defending the second group of outlaws, the drug-traffickers, from attack by the authorities. This deal was, however, abandoned after the traffickers, who had pretensions to respectability and social acceptance and had become big landowners, realised that the Marxists were their enemy.

Almost all-powerful

By the late 1980s the notorious Medellin and Cali cartels had become almost unstoppable. They could buy most officials or terrify them into submission to their will. They ordered the assassinations of cabinet ministers, judges, journalists, generals and, in the case of Luis Carlos Galan, a front-running presidential candidate. They had teams of specially trained "executioners", adept as marksmen and at planting bombs. They owned football teams, chain stores and, it was said, prominent politicians. The runway at Cali airport was said to re-open at night for drug flights. The wealth of the cartels, and their ruthlessness, seemed boundless. Nonetheless, one of the Medellin bosses, Carlos Lehder, was extradited to America, tried and jailed. In 1989 a leading figure, Gonzalo Rodriguez Gacha, was killed in a shoot-out. The chief of the cartel, Pablo Escobar, was captured and detained, under a special deal, in a newly fitted jail in 1991. He escaped in 1992, to the acute embarrassment of the government, but was killed in a shoot-out in 1993. The government claimed that, having beaten Medellin's cartel, it would go after Cali's. But the alleged Cali leader, Gilberto Rodriguez Orejuela, was a more discreet operator than the rash men from Medellin.

Patient, risky and often tedious negotiations by the government with guerrilla gangs had results. In 1986 the Patriotic Union, the political wing of the FARC, won seats in both houses of Congress. In 1989 the M-19 group laid down its arms and became a political party. These were brave men and women: two Patriotic Union presidential candidates, several congressmen and many local-government politicians were murdered in cold blood by right-wing paramilitary thugs, some of them linked to rich landowners. One of the ex-guerrillas prospered: Antonio Navarro Wolf of M-19 served as a health minister and as a prominent member of a constituent assembly. He too had presidential ambitions. By 1993 only three groups were still active.

Politics: strands of hope

The 1957 agreement which ended The Violence lasted until 1974 when, for the first time, the presidency did not alternate from the outgoing Liberal head of state to a Conservative. The change passed peacefully. A Liberal candidate won again in 1978 and a Conservative won in 1982. Substantive change began with the Liberal President Virgilio Barco (1986–90). The Conservatives declined his unenthusiastic offer of seats in the cabinet and entered the congressional opposition for the first time in 30 years. The country's mayors, hitherto appointed by the president, were elected. The government had long been seen as the preserve of a rich landowning oligarchy associated with a small band of industrialists (nestling behind high tariff walls). The vast majority of Colombians felt alienated. Few bothered to vote.

Opening time

After President Barco was succeeded by another Liberal, the young and dynamic Cesar Gaviria, Colombia began to change more rapidly. Mr Gaviria convened a constituent assembly to open up Colombian politics. Elections for state governors, hitherto appointed, were held for the first time. Large official allocations of money to sitting members of Congress, helping them to win re-election, were abolished. Mr Gaviria was succeeded, in an election in June 1994, by another Liberal, Ernesto Samper, who narrowly defeated the Conservative, Andres Pastrana, amid allegations that drug money might have been used in the campaigns.

Society: troubled inheritance

The curse of violence has not yet been lifted. It may never be: this is a big country full of remote towns and villages where hard men settle accounts directly, where feuds are not forgotten and where many people have access to guns. However, as politics and the economy open up, and the country achieves stability, the violence ought to diminish. It would be reassuring if, as a first proof that the change is having an effect, more people voted. The turnout in 1994 was 55%. The sense of alienation will, however, be lifted only after the poor people detect an unmistakeable improvement in their standard of living.

The economy: steady evolution

For decades Colombia's economy was based on coffee. In the past decade, however, it has diversified. It has the makings of a prosperous country. There is a big newly discovered oil deposit at Cusiana which BP is exploiting. There is a huge deposit of coal at El Cerrejon which is being exported. Colombia has great hydroelectric power potential which is now being slowly exploited. It is, however, still mainly an agricultural country. In addition to coffee, it produces bananas on the north coast (some of the crop being produced by ex-guerrillas), sugar (around Cali in the Cauca valley), cotton and cut flowers (a booming non-traditional export). Some coca and marijuana is grown, but the traffickers mainly work with imports from Peru and Bolivia which are re-exported to America and Europe. The country industrialised slowly with textiles leading the way. Finance ministers pursued a prudent course, avoiding heavy indebtedness. Colombia did not have to reschedule its debt during the crisis of the 1980s. Ministers concentrated on trying to reduce inflation from the usual 20–30% but this often meant reining in potentially inflationary economic growth. The country enjoyed modest economic growth but it was not much more than population growth, and the increase was distributed unequally.

The big shake-up

President Gaviria slashed import tariffs, obliging firms to meet international competition and encouraging them to export. He broke with traditional caution and welcomed foreign investment. He privatised state enterprises including banks. He signed a historic free-trade agreement with Venezuela that was subsequently extended to Ecuador, and separate free-trade agreements with Chile, Mexico and the Central American countries. The first of these agreements quickly produced a sharp increase in regional trade. With its political and economic opening, Colombia was entering a new stage of its troubled history. Without its traffickers and its guerrillas, it would be well on the road to prosperity.

Total area	1,138,914 sq km	% agricultural area	35
Capital	Bogota	Highest point metres	Colon 5,800
Other cities	Medellin, Cali, Barranquilla	Main rivers	Magdalena

The economy

GDP $bn	44.6	GDP per head $	1,330
% av. ann. growth in real GDP 1987–92	3.5	GDP per head in purchasing power parity (USA=100)	24.7

Origins of GDP	*% of total*	**Components of GDP**	*% of total*
Agriculture	16	Private consumption	67
Industry	35	Public consumption	12
of which:		Investment	18
manufacturing	20	Exports	19
Services	49	Imports	-16

Structure of manufacturing

			% of total
Agric. & food processing	30	Other	45
Textiles & clothing	15	Av. ann. increase in industrial	
Machinery & transport	10	output 1987–90	3.5

Inflation and exchange rates

Consumer price 1993 av. ann. incr.	22%	Pesos per $ av. 1993	863.1
Av. ann. rate 1988–93	28.1%	Pesos per ecu av. 1993	966.7

Balance of payments, reserves, aid and debt

			$bn
Visible exports fob	7.3	Capital balance	0.3
Visible imports fob	-6.0	Overall balance	1.2
Trade balance	1.3	Change in reserves	1.2
Invisible inflows	2.4	Level of reserves end Dec.	7.6
Invisible outflows	-2.8	Foreign debt	17.2
Net transfers	1.7	as % of GDP	36.7
Current account balance	0.9	Debt service	
as % of GDP	2.0	as % of export earnings	35.3

Principal exports	*$bn fob*	**Principal imports**	*$bn cif*
Oil & oil products	1.4	Intermediate goods	3.3
Coffee	1.3	Capital goods	2.2
Coal	0.5	Consumer goods	0.9
Gold	0.4	Fuel	0.3

Main export destinations	*% of total*	**Main origins of imports**	*% of total*
USA	39.2	USA	38.5
Venezuela	8.5	Japan	7.4
Germany	8.5	Venezuela	6.7
Netherlands	3.9	Germany	6.3
Peru	3.5	Brazil	4.0

Government

System Republic with dominant executive branch. Bicameral Congress consisting of nationally elected Senate and House of Representatives.
Main political parties Liberal Party, Social Conservative Party, M-19 Democratic Alliance

Climate and topography

Tropical along coast and eastern plains, cooler in highlands. Flat coastal lowlands, central highlands, high Andes mountains and eastern lowland plains.

People and society

Population m	33.4	% under 15	32.9
Pop. per sq km	31	% over 65	4.5
% urban	70	No. men per 100 women	100
% av. ann. growth 1987–92	2.4	Human Development Index	77.0
No. households m	5.6		

Life expectancy	*yrs*	**Education**	
Men	66	Spending as % of GDP	2.9
Women	72	Years of compulsory education	...
Crude birth rate	24.0	Adult literacy %	87
Crude death rate	6.0	Primary school enrolment %	73
Infant mortality		Secondary school enrolment %	52
per 1,000 live births	...	Tertiary education enrolment %	14

Workforce	*% of total*	**Consumer goods ownership**	
			Pop. per
Services	68		
Industry	31	Car	35.7
Agriculture	1	TV	8.7
% unemployed	10.0	Telephone	12.3

Ethnic groups	*% of total*	**Religious groups**	*% of total*
Mestizo	58	Roman Catholic	95
White	20		
Mulatto	14		
Black	4		

Tourism		**Health**	
Tourist arrivals m	0.8	Pop. per doctor	1,230
Tourist receipts $bn	0.4		

ECUADOR

Total area	283,560 sq km	Population	10.7m
GDP	$11.8bn	GDP per head	$1,070
Capital	Quito	Other cities	Guayaquil

For most of its history, Ecuador has been a poor backwater ruled by generals or strongmen. Since 1987, however, its democracy has been consolidated and since 1992 it has moved steadily down the road to free-market economic policies.

History: lost lands

When discovered by Spain in 1530 Ecuador was ruled by the Incas. For the Spaniards, it was of little significance. It has remained neglected. There have been exceptions, however. After independence in 1820, more powerful neighbours tried to grab parts of its territory. Ecuador lost two wars with Colombia, one with Brazil and, in 1941, one with Peru which ended with the loss of one province and part of another.

Politics: give me a balcony

Ecuador has had a volatile, unstable and occasionally melodramatic political life. Presidents have frequently lacked a majority in Congress, which has frequently been fractious. In the 19th century the trouble was between pro-Church conservatives and anti-clerical liberals. In the 20th century it was devoted mostly to personal rivalries, with occasional challenges to the twin establishment: the government in Quito, the inland capital, and merchants based in Guayaquil, the main port and commercial capital of the country. The most theatrical, and probably most loved, of Ecuador's presidents was the mercurial Jose Maria Velasco Ibarra, a brilliant orator and populist. Mr Velasco used to say, not entirely inaccurately: "Give me a balcony and I will be president!" The trouble was that the army and the establishment regarded him as a firebrand. He was elected president in 1934, 1944, 1952, 1960 and 1968, and was allowed to serve only one full term.

Slowing down and speeding up

The armed forces held power from 1963 to 1966 and from 1972 to 1979, when democracy returned and was consolidated. Leon Febres Cordero (1984–88), a conservative, excitable and impatient populist with an authoritarian streak who had been a businessman in New Jersey, propelled the country towards economic liberalism and welcomed foreign investment. Rodrigo Borja (1988–92) swung the country back to social democracy and reforms through *gradualismo*. Ecuador altered course again under Sixto Duran, a veteran politician with backing from the establishments in both Quito and Guayaquil, who took office in 1992. Mr Duran advocated a speed-up of economic reforms and, although he did not enjoy a majority in Congress, won approval for some.

Society: class, race and geography

There is a small ruling class, a small but growing middle class and a large number of peasants, many of whom speak local languages and survive on small-scale subsistence farming. Ecuador is also divided between formal Quito, nestling in a fold of the Andes near the slopes of a volcano, and the more informal yet frenetic traders of Guayaquil on the coast.

The economy: unexploited hills

Commercial agriculture employs roughly a third of the workforce, mostly along the coast, where bananas, rice, coffee, cocoa and sugar are grown. In recent years shrimp-farming has boomed. More than half of the country's export earnings, however, come from oil. In 1986 part of Ecuador was hit by an earthquake which cut the pipeline taking oil to a coastal terminal until the next year. Natural gas has been discovered offshore. Most of Ecuador's electricity supply will come from dams now built or being planned. Large deposits of gold and copper have been found.

Freer trade

In October 1993 Congress approved a framework bill allowing Mr Duran to privatise, deregulate and open up the economy. He took Ecuador into a free-trade area with Colombia and Venezuela in the same year. But an attempt to increase oil prospecting ran into trouble from ecologists who criticised Texaco for causing environmental damage. A plan to privatise the state oil company, PetroEcuador, ran into trouble from trade unionists, ecologists and anthropologists, and was watered down. The president's own position was being undermined by the vice-president, Alberto Dahik, who, at the end of 1993, was said to be running the country on a day-to-day basis. GDP growth in 1993 was only 1.5%, less than the rate of population growth.

Total area	283,560 sq km	% agricultural area	26
Capital	Quito	Highest point metres	Chimborazo
Other cities	Guayaquil, Cuenca		6,265

The economy

GDP $bn	11.8	GDP per head $	1,070
% av. ann. growth in real GDP 1987–92	4.4	GDP per head in purchasing power parity (USA=100)	18.7

Origins of GDP	*% of total*	**Components of GDP**	*% of total*
Agriculture	15	Private consumption	70
Industry	35	Public consumption	8
of which:		Investment	22
manufacturing	21	Exports	31
Services	50	Imports	-28

Structure of manufacturing

			% of total
Agric. & food processing	31	Other	50
Textiles & clothing	13	Av. ann. increase in industrial output 1987–92	...
Machinery & transport	7		

Inflation and exchange rates

Consumer price 1993 av. ann. incr.	45.0%	Sucres per $ av. 1993	1,945.2
Av. ann. rate 1987–93	54.1%	Sucres per ecu av. 1993	2,178.6

Balance of payments[a], reserves, aid and debt

			$bn
Visible exports fob	-2.9	Capital balance	-1.3
Visible imports fob	2.2	Overall balance	-0.9
Trade balance	0.6	Change in reserves	0.09
Invisible inflows	0.6	Level of reserves end Dec.	0.9
Invisible outflows	-1.8	Foreign debt	12.3
Net transfers	...	as % of GDP	102.1
Current account balance	-0.5	Debt service	
as % of GDP	-0.1	as % of export earnings	27.1

Principal exports	*$bn fob*	**Principal imports**	*$bn cif*
Oil & oil products	1.3	Industrial supplies	0.8
Bananas	0.6	Capital goods	0.5
Shrimp	0.5	Transport equipment	0.3
Coffee	0.1	Consumer goods	0.2

Main export destinations	*% of total*	**Main origins of imports**	*% of total*
USA	42.0	USA	33.8
Germany	5.6	Japan	12.3
South Korea	5.4	Germany	6.5
Chile	4.5	Colombia	4.4

Government

System Republic with president elected directly by universal suffrage for non-renewable 4-year term. Unicameral 71-member National Congress.
Main political parties Social Christian Party, Conservative Party

Climate and topography

Tropical along coast with cooler interior. Coastal plain (*costa*), inter-Andean central highlands (*sierra*) and flat-to-rolling eastern jungle (*oriente*).

People and society

Population m	10.7	% under 15	39.5
Pop. per sq km	38	% over 65	3.6
% urban	56	No. men per 100 women	102
% av. ann. growth 1987–92	2.4	Human Development Index	64.6
No. households m	2.5		

Life expectancy	*yrs*	**Education**	
Men	67	Spending as % of GDP	2.7
Women	72	Years of compulsory education	7
Crude birth rate	28	Adult literacy %	86
Crude death rate	6	Primary school enrolment %	...
Infant mortality		Secondary school enrolment %	56
per 1,000 live births	42	Tertiary education enrolment %	29

Workforce	*% of total*	**Consumer goods ownership**	
			Pop. per
Services	46		
Industry	24	Car	66.7
Agriculture	30	TV	12.0
% unemployed	8.9	Telephone	27.8

Ethnic groups	*% of total*	**Religious groups**	*% of total*
Mestizo	55	Roman Catholic	95
Indian	25		
Spanish	10		
Black	10		

Tourism		**Health**	
Tourist arrivals m	0.3	Pop. per doctor	820
Tourist receipts $bn	0.2		

a 1991.

FRENCH GUIANA

French Guiana is best known for its notorious detention centre on Devil's Island, where prisoners, many of them political, used to mingle freely with citizens because there was no means of escape. The penal colony was closed in 1937. In more modern times, French Guiana has achieved respectability as the home of the launching pad for the European space satellite, Ariane.

History: consistent neglect

For decades French Guiana was neglected by the French government but nothing much happened. In the 1970s, however, demonstrations in favour of more autonomy or outright independence erupted. In 1980 and 1983 supporters of independence detonated bombs at government offices. The French government arrested some of the separatists and announced plans for economic development. Not much came of the latter except the space base at Kourou.

Politics: Socialists under pressure

The French government is represented by a prefect. In the regional council the Guiana Socialist Party, at the head of a coalition, became divided in the late 1980s amid allegations of corruption and lost ground in the 1992 election. It survived in office, with a majority of one, led by Antoine Karam.

Society: ethnic mixture

Most of the population is black or American Indian. There are, however, settlements of Hmong farmers from Laos. The troubles in neighbouring Suriname have encouraged thousands of Surinamese to cross the border illegally and settle under the security of the French flag. The space centre has brought in thousands of scientists who live in a community of their own. They are paid and spend well. It is a potentially explosive mixture.

The economy: under-developed

Although French Guiana receives large annual subsidies, it remains under-developed and the trade deficit is large. The biggest exports are shrimps and timber. There is little tourism. Enough sugar cane is cut to keep a rum distillery going. The potential for agricultural development and hydroelectric energy is considerable.

Total area	91,000 sq km	Highest point metres	Tumac-Humac 700
Capital	Cayenne	Main rivers	Carnopi, Inini, Maroinjne

Government

System Overseas department of France, administered by directly elected General Council and Regional Council. Represented in French National Assembly by 2 deputies and one senator.
Main political parties Guiana Socialist Party, Rally for the Republic, Guiana Democratic Action

Climate and topography

Tropical; hot and humid with little seasonal variation in temperature. Low-lying coastal plains rising to hills and small mountains.

People and society

Population	10,000	% under 15	...
Pop. per sq km	0.1	% over 65	...
% urban	...	No. men per 100 women	...
% av. ann. growth 1987–92	nil	No. households m	...
Human Development Index	...		

Ethnic groups	*% of total*	**Religious groups**	*% of total*
Black or mulatto	66	Predominantly Roman Catholic	
White	12		
East Indian, Chinese or Amerindian	12		
Other	10		

GUYANA

Total area	214,970 sq km	Population	810,000
GDP	$268m	GDP per head	$330
Capital	Georgetown	Other cities	New Amsterdam, Linden

With a large land area for a small population, Guyana should prosper. But for 19 years misguided policies and a politician's greed for power have blocked progress. The result is that most Guyanans are poor. There is, however, a glimmer of hope.

History: divided country

Since the 17th century the Guyana area had been developed by Dutch colonisers who drained the swamps and cultivated sugar for export with the help of slaves imported from Africa and indentured labourers from China, India and Portugal. The territory became British in 1816 and was known as British Guiana. Since the end of the second world war Guyana's history has been overshadowed by the rivalry of two men: Forbes Burnham, a radical black lawyer from a middle-class family, and Cheddi Jagan, a Marxist, American-educated dentist and son of an Indian cane-cutter. The two men worked together to form the People's Progressive Party (PPP) in 1950.

Three years later the PPP easily won a general election to form a pre-independence government and announced radical policies. Britain, prompted by anti-communist American politicians, closed the House of Assembly and replaced it with an appointed legislature. After this setback, disputes over policy led Burnham and Jagan to split; Burnham formed the black-dominated People's National Congress (PNC) while Jagan's PPP became a strong voice in the Indian community. The British and Americans were determined to keep Jagan out of power. Britain agreed to Guyana's independence only after its introduction of proportional representation in 1963 paved the way for an election that was won by the PNC in alliance with a small conservative group. Independence was granted in 1966 with Burnham as prime minister.

Politics: what fraud?

For the next 19 years Burnham remained in power, disregarding widespread complaints of electoral fraud. In 1970 he proclaimed Guyana to be a "Co-operative Republic" with himself as president. In 1979 the leader of a small political party was killed by a bomb and the PPP's offices were attacked by arsonists. Many people blamed the PNC. Most opposition parties boycotted elections in 1980.

The economy: Guyana sinks

Under Burnham, most of the economy including the bauxite company and sugar plantations were nationalised and mismanaged. The Co-operative Republic slid into penury. It could not service debts to the World Bank and the IMF. Its foreign debt totalled more than $1 billion. There was no new investment and no job creation (except by the government). Many young Guyanans who had received a good education emigrated.

Burnham was succeeded on his death in 1985 by the vice-president, Desmond Hoyte, who had become a convert to IMF policies, including a state-sector wage freeze. Mr Hoyte won a general election in 1986. (The opposition said it was fraudulent and boycotted local elections in 1989.) Mr Hoyte said he wanted to "roll back co-operative socialism". He restored relations with and obtained loans from the IMF, the World Bank and the Inter-American Development Bank. He established good relations with the United States. He brought in Booker and Tate & Lyle to manage the sugar plantations. Rice production improved and an ambitious start was made to logging. Foreign bauxite companies were invited to manage a company nationalised with disastrous results by Burnham and to exploit deposits in a joint venture. There were also plans for big investments in gold and diamond mining in the south. It was a considerable achievement by Mr Hoyte, and required bravery. But would the president play fair with the opposition?

Jagan wins

He had no alternative. His adversaries placed their hopes on the presidential and parliamentary election in 1990. Independent and opposition members were appointed to the Elections Commission. But preparation of an honest and reliable voters' roll caused long and suspicious delays. Buoyed by signs that Guyana's long recession was ending, Mr Hoyte had high hopes of winning. But his union friends, opposed to the unpopular IMF austerity policies, deserted him. A fair election was held in 1992 and the opposition won with 55% of the vote. Cheddi Jagan's long struggle for power had finally succeeded. The new president, aged 74, was in danger of seeming an anachronism. But he had changed, like Mr Hoyte, and was more likely to follow the teachings of the IMF than those of Karl Marx.

Total area	214,970 sq km	% agricultural area	9
Capital	Georgetown	Highest point metres	Mount Roraima 2,772
Other cities	New Amsterdam, Linden	Main rivers	Potaro, Essequibo, Demarera

The economy

GDP $m	268	GDP per head $	330
% av. ann. growth in real GDP 1987–92	0.6	GDP per head in purchasing power parity (USA=100)	...

Origins of GDP	*% of total*	**Components of GDP**	*% of total*
Agriculture	50	Private consumption	52
Industry	26	Public consumption	14
of which:		Investment	32
manufacturing	4	Exports	87
Services	24	Imports	-84

Structure of manufacturing

% of total

Agric. & food processing	...	Other	...
Textiles & clothing	...	Av. ann. increase in industrial	
Machinery & transport	...	output 1987–92	...

Inflation and exchange rates

Consumer price 1992 av. ann. incr.	2.5%	Guyana $ per $ av. 1993	130.8
Av. ann. rate 1987–92	9.6%	Guyana $ per ecu av. 1993	146.5

Balance of payments, reserves, aid and debt

$m

Visible exports fob	313	Capital balance	...
Visible imports fob	285	Overall balance	...
Trade balance	28	Change in reserves	...
Invisible inflows	...	Level of reserves end Dec.	188
Invisible outflows	...	Foreign debt	1,879
Net transfers	...	as % of GDP	501
Current account balance	-0.07	Debt service	
as % of GDP	-0.1	as % of export earnings	...

Principal exports	*$m fob*	**Principal imports**	*$m cif*
Sugar	134	Capital goods	135
Bauxite & alumina	57	Fuels & lubricants	67
Rice	35	Consumer goods	59

Main export destinations	*% of total*	**Main origins of imports**	*% of total*
UK	32.9	USA	36.7
USA	30.5	Trinidad & Tobago	12.6
Canada	8.7	UK	11.0
France	4.9	Italy	8.1
Japan	3.2	Japan	4.4

Government

System Co-operative republic. National Assembly consists of 65 elected members. Whole of country forms one electoral area; voters cast votes for a party list of candidates.

Main political parties People's National Congress, People's Progressive Party, Working People's Alliance

Climate and topography

Tropical; hot and humid with two rainy seasons, May to mid-August and mid-November to mid-January. Mostly rolling highlands with savannah in south.

People and society

Population	810,000	% under 15	34.6
Pop. per sq km	4	% over 65	4.1
% urban	35	No. men per 100 women	100
% av. ann. growth 1987–92	0.5	No. households m	...
Human Development Index	54.1		

Life expectancy	*yrs*	**Education**	
Men	66	Spending as % of GDP	8.8
Women	71	Years of compulsory education	...
Crude birth rate	25	Adult literacy %	98
Crude death rate	7	Primary school enrolment %	...
Infant mortality		Secondary school enrolment %	64
per 1,000 live births	36	Tertiary education enrolment %	4

Workforce	*% of total*	**Consumer goods ownership**	
Services	47		*Pop. per*
Industry	26	Car	...
Agriculture	27	TV	2,510
% unemployed	...	Telephone	...

Ethnic groups	*% of total*	**Religious groups**	*% of total*
East Indian	51	Christian	57
Black/mixed	43	Hindu	33
Amerindian	4	Muslim	9
European and Chinese	2	Other	1

Tourism		**Health**	
Tourist arrivals m	...	Pop. per doctor	6,200
Tourist receipts $bn	...		

PARAGUAY

Total area	406,750 sq km	Population	4.5m
GDP	$6.0bn	GDP per head	$1,340
Capital	Asuncion	Other cities	Presidenta Stroessner, Pedro Juan Caballero

Paraguay is a remote, land-locked country well off the beaten track. The official language is Spanish but most people also speak guarani, the regional Amerindian language. Since independence in 1814, Paraguay has been mostly ruled by despots and their flunkeys. Its rulers have enriched themselves and the government's coffers since the end of the second world war by smuggling large quantities of untaxed cigarettes and liquor across its neighbours' borders. Slowly Paraguay is joining the 20th century. It has its first civilian president in its 180-year history. Two opposition parties control Congress.

History: a tale of four bosses

After independence Paraguay fell under the dictatorial rule of Gaspar Rodriguez de Francia and then Carlos Antonio Lopez and his son, Francisco. This lasted until 1870, giving the country stability unmatched in the region. In 1864, Lopez the younger embroiled Paraguay in a war against Argentina, Brazil and Uruguay, which proved a disaster: when it ended in 1870 the population had been halved. Paraguay did rather better in its Chaco War with Bolivia which ended in 1935, gaining a large part of the Chaco region as booty. But the land was mainly arid and infertile.

The general knew best

Paraguay's fourth boss was General Alfredo Stroessner, who seized power in 1954 during a period of political ferment. The son of a German father and a Paraguayan mother, General Stroessner held power until he was deposed in a bloodless coup 35 years later. Like the 19th century strongmen, he had given Paraguay a remarkable period of stability. However, not much social progress was achieved under him: the Colorado Party, to which he was aligned, the wealthy landowners and the army's officer corps did well; the landless rural peasants did not. About half of the population lives in poverty. General Stroessner was ousted by General Antonio Rodriguez, who became popular for having removed the dictator even though he was a general and a Colorado. A degree of respect for civil rights was restored, partly as a result of pressure by the United States. President Rodriguez stepped down at the end of his term (albeit unenthusiastically) as the new constitution required.

Politics: a divided opposition

As the next presidential election approached, the Colorados split over their candidate. But the opposition, active as never before, failed to form an essential electoral alliance. As a result the election in March 1993 was won by the official candidate, Juan Carlos Wasmosy, a 54-year-old ethnic Hungarian businessman who deals in cotton and property, with 40% of the vote. The veteran democratic opposition leader, Domingo Laino, came second with 32% and a wealthy moderate businessman, Guillermo Caballero, was third with 24%.

The fact that the election was held at all, and that such a result was achieved, was a sign of modest progress for Paraguay. It did, however, leave the power structure intact (apart from the opposition-controlled Congress). Nonetheless, a united opposition might just win the next presidential election. It should not be forgotten, however, that the powerful commander of the first army corps based outside Asuncion, General Lino Oviedo, said in 1993 that the army and the Colorado Party would, between them, run Paraguay "forever". However, in order to ensure the passage of legislation, government and opposition formed a "pact of governability". This meant that the opposition would be consulted before the government proposed legislation. In the early 1990s the political life of quiet Asuncion was effervescent with strikes, demonstrations and protest marches.

The economy: excessive prudence

While other Latin American countries sank into a debt crisis in the 1980s, Paraguay preserved a relatively low-debt, low-inflation (20% in 1993) economy. The trouble was that it grew more slowly than the population, although that situation was reversed in 1993 when the economy grew at about 4% and the population at 3%. It will never be easy to attract investors to this backwater and pull it out of poverty. Under General Rodriguez, Paraguay began to open up its economy to the world in deals with International Monetary Fund and foreign government creditors. But it was fragile and unbalanced: in 1993 only about 6% of the budget went on capital expenditure. Mr Wasmosy and his finance minister, Crispiniano Sandoval, were committed to pressing on with free-market reforms and to strengthening the free-trade area with Brazil, Argentina and Uruguay (Mercosul).

Total area	406,750 sq km	% agricultural area	60
Capital	Asuncion	Main rivers	Paraguay, Pilcomayo
Other cities	Presidenta Stroessner, Pedro Juan Caballero		

The economy

GDP $bn	6.0	GDP per head $	1,340
% av. ann. growth in real GDP 1987–91	4.4	GDP per head in purchasing power parity (USA=100)	15.5

Origins of GDP	*% of total*	**Components of GDP**	*% of total*
Agriculture	22	Private consumption	75
Industry	24	Public consumption	8
of which:		Investment	25
manufacturing	18	Exports	26
Services	54	Imports	-32

Structure of manufacturing

			% of total
Agric. & food processing	...	Other	...
Textiles & clothing	...	Av. ann. increase in industrial	
Machinery & transport	...	output 1987–92	...

Inflation and exchange rates

Consumer price 1992 av. ann. incr.	15.2%	Guaranies per $ av. 1993	1,744.3
Av. ann. rate 1987–92	25.1%	Guaranies per ecu av. 1993	1,953.6

Balance of payments, reserves, aid and debt

			$bn
Visible exports fob	1.0	Capital balance	0.2
Visible imports fob	-1.5	Overall balance	...
Trade balance	-0.5	Change in reserves	-0.4
Invisible inflows	0.7	Level of reserves end Dec.	0.5
Invisible outflows	-0.7	Foreign debt	1.7
Net transfers	0.1	as % of GDP	27.8
Current account balance	-0.4	Debt service	
as % of GDP	-6.6	as % of export earnings	40.9

Principal exports	*$m fob*	**Principal imports**	*$m cif*
Soybeans	229	Machinery	427
Cotton	160	Vehicles & parts	153
Timber	68	Fuels & lubricants	130
Hides & skins	59	Beverages & tobacco	111

Main export destinations	*% of total*	**Main origins of imports**	*% of total*
Brazil	28.3	Brazil	21.3
Netherlands	18.1	Argentina	16.2
Argentina	7.6	Japan	13.6
France	5.9	USA	11.5

Government

System Republic. President directly elected for 5-year (renewable) term. Bicameral Congress. President has powers to rule by decree when Congress is in recess.

Main political parties Colorado Party, Authentic Radical Liberal Party, National Encounter

Climate and topography

Varies from temperate in east to semi-arid in far west. Grassy plains and wooded hills west of Paraguay river. Low, marshy plain near river. Forest elsewhere.

People and society

Population m	4.5	% under 15	41.1
Pop. per sq km	11	% over 65	3.5
% urban	48	No. men per 100 women	103
% av. ann. growth 1987–92	2.9	Human Development Index	64.1
No. households m	...		

Life expectancy	*yrs*	**Education**	
Men	71	Spending as % of GDP	1.0
Women	74	Years of compulsory education	6
Crude birth rate	33	Adult literacy %	90
Crude death rate	5	Primary school enrolment %	95
Infant mortality		Secondary school enrolment %	30
per 1,000 live births	28	Tertiary education enrolment %	8

Workforce	*% of total*	**Consumer goods ownership**	
			Pop. per
Services	31		
Industry	21	Car	...
Agriculture	48	TV	16.9
% unemployed	6.0	Telephone	37.0

Ethnic groups	*% of total*	**Religious groups**	*% of total*
Mestizo	95	Roman Catholic	90
White or Indian	5	Mennonite and other Protestants	10

Tourism		**Health**	
Tourist arrivals m	0.3	Pop. per doctor	1,460
Tourist receipts $bn	0.1		

PERU

Total area	1,285,216 sq km	Population	22.3m
GDP	$21.3bn	GDP per head	$950
Capital	Lima	Other cities	Arequipa, Callao, Trujillo

Peru is a tragic country which, after long years of misgovernment and appalling social injustice, is slowly rising from the ashes. It has a firm government applying sound economic policies and achieving remarkable results. The trouble is that President Alberto Fujimori, though standing tall in the opinion polls, lacks full legitimacy.

History: an odd sophistication

In 1500 the Inca empire, based in Peru, spread from what was later to become Colombia in the north to Chile in the south. Agriculture was relatively advanced; terracing and irrigation were elaborate. A network of roads was used to bring produce to market. But there was no wheel, no plough, no coinage and no written language. However, rich deposits of gold and silver were mined and turned into beautiful ornaments.

Cruel visitors

Into this remote civilisation erupted one of the roughest and least principled of the conquistadors, Francisco Pizarro. First Pizarro captured and garrotted Atahualpa, king of what had become a divided realm. Then, moving south, he grabbed the rest and established his capital at Lima in 1535; the town subsequently became the headquarters of a Spanish viceroy.

Unchanged balance

The invaders seized the indigenous population's land and subjugated the people, who were placed under great pressure to abandon their ancient beliefs and espouse Christianity (which they duly did). A small Spanish population ruled a huge Indian one, with a considerable degree of ruthlessness. In 1782 an Indian leader, Tupac Amaru, united various ethnic groups in opposing Spanish rule. In subsequent fighting, thousands of Indians were killed and Tupac Amaru, who fell into the hands of the Spaniards, was torn limb from limb by horses in the square at Cuzco. The colonial experience left wounds in Peruvian society which are unhealed today.

Haya was kept out of power

Independence from Spain came in 1824 after rebel forces defeated the royal army at the Battle of Ayacucho. A period of instability led to rule by military strongmen, although the country lived under democratic rule from 1885 to 1919. The ethnic Spanish establishment received its first serious democratic challenge with the formation of the left-wing, nationalist American Popular Revolutionary Alliance (APRA) in 1924, under the charismatic Victor Raul Haya de la Torre, who was a towering figure in Peruvian politics for five decades. The establishment, acting at times through the generals, kept APRA from power by various subterfuges.

Politics: a democratic disappointment

Genuine democracy was planted in Peru with the election in 1963 of Fernando Belaunde, a visionary and somewhat impractical architect-politician with little interest in the detailed running of government. Mr Belaunde dreamed of linking up the remote interior by a highway. He paid little heed to improving Peru's economy or to improving the (low) quality of government in general. Mr Belaunde was ousted in 1968 by the army chief of staff, General Juan Velasco Alvarado, who embarked on an unusual experiment in military socialism: land reform and sweeping nationalisation was combined with a muzzling of the media and an attempt to improve the lot of slum-dwellers. The experiment, unique in Latin America at the time, undermined Peru's power structure, but failed. The general was ousted and a presidential election in 1981 brought Mr Belaunde back to power.

Rise of the terrorists

By this time the economy, always weak, was in tatters and a ruthless new guerrilla group, Shining Path (Sendero Luminoso), taking its inspiration from China's Mao Zedong, was murdering its way to power and influence in the interior. Mr Belaunde had learned nothing. As ineffectual as ever, he stayed on until elections in 1985 which were won by the opposition APRA candidate, the young, handsome and charismatic successor to Haya de la Torre, Alan Garcia. Unfortunately, Mr Garcia was also a disaster. A military campaign to eliminate Shining Path, during which human rights were frequently violated by scared and brutal policemen and soldiers, failed.

Rise of inflation

Mr Garcia tried to revive an economy that was operating much under capacity. At first it responded well: GDP grew remarkably and inflation did not take off. But too much money was chasing too few goods. Inflation shot upwards and Peru's tax-collecting capacity, poor at best, was not up to the job of working in a highly inflationary environment. Budget deficits became huge and Mr Garcia printed money to cover them. Inflation slipped out of control. The condition of the poor living in slums around Lima and the port city of Callao became desperate. Crime became endemic and the only growth industry was the employment of security guards. Mr Garcia grew desperate and sought favour with populist actions. He decided to nationalise the banks. At one point he sent a tank to batter down the big front door of a recalcitrant bank in the city centre. The photograph was published around the world. Peru's reputation, and that of Mr Garcia, were in tatters. It was one of the worst moments in Peru's tragic history.

"El Chino" takes over

Mr Garcia was succeeded in 1990 by Alberto Fujimori, a Peruvian of Japanese origin yet popularly known as "El Chino", whose vague policy platform was more attractive than the rigorous IMF-style reforms advocated by the conservative candidate, Mario Vargas Llosa, Peru's most famous novelist. Mr Fujimori won and promptly applied his opponent's policies. He started off with sweeping privatisations. In 1992, frustrated at what he saw as inaction by Congress and corruption in the courts, Mr Fujimori closed Congress, set up a government of emergency and national reconstruction and fired 13 of the 28 Supreme Court judges in order to "prevent the country's collapse". This met with international disapproval and Mr Fujimori convened a constituent assembly and held congressional elections that were mostly boycotted by the opposition. His standing in the opinion polls, always high, was boosted by a revival of the economy and the capture in 1992 of the leader of Shining Path, Abimael Guzman, who unexpectedly issued a call from jail for internal peace. In October 1993 Mr Fujimori narrowly won a referendum on a new constitution, allowing him to seek re-election.

Society: divided

Although there has been much intermarriage, Peru is populated mostly by indigenous people or those of mixed origin and ruled mostly by people of ethnic Spanish origin. Millions of indigenous people have become absorbed by Hispanic culture since Pizarro's time; others continue to speak Quechua and Aymara. Most Peruvians are Catholic but, as in many parts of the region, there is a resurgence of Protestantism.

The economy: drugs and anchovies

The most important export is illegal: coca leaves, to make cocaine for the American and European market. Poor Peruvians have always chewed coca leaves to dull the pangs of hunger; now they sell them for what is, for them, a fortune. Nobody knows how big the market is: one estimate, of $3 billion a year, is almost certainly much too high. Anti-drugs campaigns have a sporadic impact, but the trade will continue as long as there is a market abroad, poverty in the countryside at home and a badly paid (and therefore corruptible) police force and army. At one time the economy depended on guano (the nitrate-rich deposits left by birds on the offshore islands). Subsequently anchovy fishing became important until stocks became depleted. Much depended on the whims of the offshore warm-water current, called El Nino, whose changes affect Peru's weather (and indeed the weather as far away as southern Africa).

Wealth in the hills

Peru is rich in minerals which might become a foundation for the economy's take-off if they created jobs and if some of the profits found their way, through the government's social policies, into investments that provided work for the poor. Apart from oil and gas there are deposits of copper, lead, zinc, silver, molybdenum, tin and iron ore.

Fujimori's reforms

By 1993 Peru's economy was back on track. Inflation had come down from 2,775% in 1988 to 48.5%. GDP, which fell in 1989 by 11.5%, grew by 6.5%. Fishing, helped by a favourable El Nino, grew by 54%, construction by 12% and manufacturing by 10%. Mining, stimulated by a newly privatised company, grew substantially. Petroleum output also grew following the signing of new exploration contracts with private companies. By June 1994 Peru's foreign-exchange reserves, which had stood at minus $150m in 1990, were worth $4.5 billion, and Peru had cleared its arrears with the IMF. Under Mr Fujimori over a billion dollars of foreign capital was invested in the Lima stock exchange. Nonetheless, unemployment is still high and wages are low. Mr Fujimori's policies had done little more than restore the economy to close to 1987 levels. He had, however, laid the essential basis for future growth. It may not have been entirely democratic, but it was a remarkable achievement.

Total area	1,285,216 sq km	% agricultural area	24
Capital	Lima	Highest point metres	Huascaran 6,760
Other cities	Arequipa, Callao, Trujillo	Main rivers	Maranon, Ucayali

The economy

GDP $bn	21.3	GDP per head $	950
% av. ann. growth in real GDP 1987–92	-5.0	GDP per head in purchasing power parity (USA=100)	14.1

Origins of GDP	*% of total*	**Components of GDP**	*% of total*
Agriculture	7	Private consumption	82
Industry	37	Public consumption	5
of which:		Investment	16
manufacturing	...	Exports	9
Services	56	Imports	-13

Structure of manufacturing

			% of total
Agric. & food processing	23	Other	53
Textiles & clothing	14	Av. ann. decrease in industrial	
Machinery & transport	10	output 1987–92	-7.8

Inflation and exchange rates

Consumer price 1993 av. ann. incr.	48.5%	New soles per $ av. 1993	1,988.3
Av. ann. rate 1988–93	460%	New soles per ecu av. 1993	2,226.9

Balance of payments, reserves, aid and debt

			$bn
Visible exports fob	3.5	Capital balance	-0.1
Visible imports fob	-4.1	Overall balance	-0.1
Trade balance	-0.6	Change in reserves	0.9
Invisible inflows	1.0	Level of reserves end Dec.	3.4
Invisible outflows	-2.8	Foreign debt	20.3
Net transfers	0.3	as % of GDP	95.4
Current account balance	-2.1	Debt service	
as % of GDP	-9.8	as % of export earnings	23.0

Principal exports	*$bn fob*	**Principal imports**	*$bn cif*
Copper	0.8	Intermediate goods	1.8
Fishmeal	0.4	Capital goods	1.1
Zinc	0.3	Consumer goods	0.8
Gold	0.2		

Main export destinations	*% of total*	**Main origins of imports**	*% of total*
USA	21.4	USA	27.2
Japan	9.9	Colombia	8.1
Italy	6.0	Argentina	5.2
Brazil	4.7	Germany	4.6

Government

System Republic. President suspended legislative and judicial branches in April 1992.

Main political parties Change 90, Popular Christian Party

Climate and topography

Varies from tropical in east to dry desert in west. Western coastal plain, rugged Andes in centre, eastern jungle in Amazon basin.

People and society

Population m	22.3	% under 15	35.5
Pop. per sq km	19	% over 65	4.1
% urban	70	No. men per 100 women	99
% av. ann. growth 1987–92	2.1	Human Development Index	59.2
No. households m	4.9		

Life expectancy	*yrs*	**Education**	
Men	63	Spending as % of GDP	3.5
Women	66	Years of compulsory education	9
Crude birth rate	29	Adult literacy %	85
Crude death rate	8	Primary school enrolment %	95
Infant mortality		Secondary school enrolment %	67
per 1,000 live births	59	Tertiary education enrolment %	...

Workforce	*% of total*	**Consumer goods ownership**	
			Pop. per
Services	53		
Industry	12	Car	52.6
Agriculture	35	TV	10.3
% unemployed	9.4	Telephone	32.3

Ethnic groups	*% of total*	**Religious groups**	*% of total*
Indian	45	Roman Catholic	95
Mestizo	37		
White	15		
Other	3		

Tourism		**Health**	
Tourist arrivals m	0.3	Pop. per doctor	1,040
Tourist receipts $bn	0.4		

SURINAME

Total area	163, 270 sq km	Population	440,000
GDP	$1.7bn	GDP per head	$3,700
Capital	Paramaribo		

Suriname, a former Dutch colony, is an interracial society in search of political and economic stability, both of which have proved to be elusive.

History: a big deal

The British founded the first settlement in what was to become Suriname at the mouth of the Suriname river in 1652 but gave it to Holland in one of the best property deals in history: a swap for New Amsterdam, the settlement at the mouth of the Hudson river that later became New York. The territory became known as Dutch Guiana, and was mostly ruled by the Dutch until independence in 1975. To work the colony's sugar plantations in the early years, the Dutch imported African slaves, many of whom ran away to the interior and were called "Bush Negroes". Later they imported indentured labourers from India, the Dutch East Indies (now Indonesia), China, Portugal and Lebanon. Many stayed and now form Suriname's unusual racial mosaic. Eventually sugar was replaced as a money-earner by bauxite and rice.

Politics: democracy was difficult

After independence the Surinamese, encouraged and financed by the Dutch, consolidated democratic rule although most of the bourgeoisie had moved to Holland to acquire a Dutch passport. Some 200,000 Surinamese are said to live in Holland. The economy deteriorated due mainly to the low world price of bauxite. In 1980 an army physical-training sergeant-major, Desi Bouterse, seized power and promoted himself to colonel. Mr Bouterse posed as a leftist and befriended Cuba's President Fidel Castro. This provoked fears in neighbouring Brazil and in the United States that Cuban influence would grow in Suriname and that the Cuban air force MIG jets would gain access to the airport at Paramaribo, Suriname's capital. From there, the MIGS could reach Venezuela and Brazil as well as numerous Caribbean islands. After two years in power, Mr Bouterse dealt ruthlessly with his growing opposition: 15 prominent politicians, trade unionists, lawyers and teachers were detained, taken to an old army fort and murdered. All western aid to Suriname was suspended.

Reverse for Bouterse

Economic pressure eventually worked: in 1987 a free election was held and a multi-racial government was formed with 40 seats in the 51-member legislature. A political party fielded by Mr Bouterse fared badly. The legislature elected a former agriculture minister, Ramsewak Shankar, as president. But the soldiers maintained a strong influence, being able to stop and question people at will and control the lucrative customs and excise. They also became a link in drug-trafficking between Colombia and the United States. In 1988 Holland resumed its aid. But in December 1990 the army ousted the president and the Dutch suspended aid again. Another election was held in May 1991 and, after a long muddle, Ronald Venetiaan, a former schoolteacher, was elected president, although Mr Bouterse still loomed in the background. Dutch aid was resumed in November 1991.

Society: a mixed bag

Roughly a third of the population is made up of "Creoles", mainly urban blacks. Another third is of American Indian origin. About 15% are Indonesian and 5% are Chinese. Each community has a political party representing its interests. The Bush Negroes rebelled against Mr Bouterse but their leader, Ronnie Brunswijk, got on better with the civilian government. At one point, however, when Mr Brunswijk came to Paramaribo to negotiate with the civilian government, the army temporarily detained him. In 1992 the guerrillas reached agreement with the government to lay down their arms in return for an amnesty for alleged human-rights abuses that also covered the army.

The economy: unstable

Under both military and civilian governments Suriname's economy has been poorly managed. In 1992 GDP fell by 5%. The fiscal deficit was 14% of GDP and covered by printing money. Inevitably, inflation was high. The government, encouraged by the Dutch, launched in 1992 a structural adjustment programme designed to cut government spending, reduce tax evasion and end import and export licensing – two procedures that were open to bribery. However, by the start of 1994 few reforms had been implemented, and the Dutch attitude to Suriname remained cautious.

Total area	163,270 sq km	% agricultural area	...
Capital	Paramaribo	Highest point metres	Juliana Top 1,230
		Main rivers	Marouijne, Correntyne, Suriname

The economy

GDP $bn	1.7	GDP per head $	3,700
% av. ann. growth in real GDP 1987–92	0.5	GDP per head in purchasing power parity (USA=100)	...

Origins of GDP	*% of total*	Components of GDP[a]	*% of total*
Agriculture	...	Private consumption	53
Industry	...	Public consumption	25
of which:		Investment	21
manufacturing	...	Exports	28
Services	...	Imports	-28

Structure of manufacturing

	% of total		
Agric. & food processing	...	Other	...
Textiles & clothing	...	Av. ann. increase in industrial	
Machinery & transport	...	output 1987–92	...

Inflation and exchange rates

Consumer price 1992 av. ann. incr.	43.7%	Guilders per $ av. 1993	1.79
Av. ann. rate 1987–92	18.9%	Guilders per ecu av. 1993	2.00

Balance of payments, reserves, aid and debt

	$bn		
Visible exports fob	0.3	Capital balance	-0.05
Visible imports fob	-0.3	Overall balance	-0.01
Trade balance	nil	Change in reserves	0.01
Invisible inflows	0.02	Level of reserves end Dec.[a]	0.02
Invisible outflows	-0.1	Foreign debt	...
Net transfers	0.03	as % of GDP	...
Current account balance	0.01	Debt service	
as % of GDP	0.6	as % of export earnings	...

Principal exports[a]	*$m fob*	Principal imports	*$m cif*
Alumina	354	...	
Aluminium	51		
Shrimps	34		
Rice	25		

Main export destinations	*% of total*	Main origins of imports	*% of total*
Norway	21.7	USA	34.0
France	20.2	Netherlands	19.9
USA	11.6	Trinidad & Tobago	10.3
Netherlands	11.4	Netherlands Antilles	6.6

Government

System Republic with unicameral National Assembly. Commander-in-Chief of the National Army maintains significant power.

Main political parties The New Front, Progressive Reform Party

Climate and topography

Tropical; moderated by trade winds. Mostly rolling hills with narrow, swampy coastal plain.

People and society

Population	440,000	% under 15	35.5
Pop. per sq km	3	% over 65	4.3
% urban	47	No. men per 100 women	97
% av. ann. growth 1987–92	1.9	Human Development Index	75.1
No. households m	...		

Life expectancy	*yrs*	**Education**	
Men	66	Spending as % of GDP	9.7
Women	71	Years of compulsory education	...
Crude birth rate	26	Adult literacy %	95
Crude death rate	6	Primary school enrolment %	100
Infant mortality		Secondary school enrolment %	53
per 1,000 live births	34	Tertiary education enrolment %	9

Workforce	*% of total*	**Consumer goods ownership**	
Services	60		*Pop. per*
Industry	20	Car	11.8
Agriculture	20	TV	7.7
% unemployed	...	Telephone	9.9

Ethnic groups	*% of total*	**Religious groups**	*% of total*
East Indian	37	Hindu	27
Creole	31	Protestant	25
Javanese	15	Roman Catholic	23
Black	10	Muslim	20
Indian	3		
Chinese	2		

Tourism		**Health**	
Tourist arrivals 000s	29	Pop. per doctor	1,260
Tourist receipts $m	11		

a 1990.

URUGUAY

Total area	176,220 sq km	Population	3.1m
GDP	$10.4bn	GDP per head	$3,340
Capital	Montevideo	Other cities	Salto, Paysandu, Las Piedras

Promoted by Britain as a small, thinly populated buffer-state between Brazil and Argentina, Uruguay became a model to Latin Americans as a welfare state. Without many natural resources, however, the country lacks the means to sustain a welfare state's high costs. It also lacks the political will to face this dilemma squarely. The result has been a decline of living standards.

History: Reds and Whites

From its discovery by Spain until independence in 1825, both Spanish and Portuguese forces held what was to become Uruguay from time to time. This led the British, who had strong commercial interests in the region and wanted to establish a stable business climate, to promote the establishment of Uruguay. But the new country was troubled by fighting and disputes between two rival groupings, the Colorados (Reds) and the Blancos (Whites). The two groups fought their last civil war in 1904. Their rivalry, now peaceful, persists today. The Blancos have become the National Party.

Politics: Batlle showed the way

In the 20th century Uruguay has been dominated by the influence of one man: Jose Batlle y Ordonez, the Colorado leader, who was president from 1903 to 1907 and from 1911 to 1916 and who towered over Uruguayan politics until his death in 1929. It was Batlle (pronounced, with an Uruguayan accent, Bajay) who introduced the welfare state. With the exception of a coup in 1933 Uruguay remained more or less democratic until 1973 when it fell under a military dictatorship that was to last until 1985. The hated regime was widely accused of torturing and killing detainees (in what it saw as a war against communist subversion). It also ruled during a period of severe recession. The return of democracy saw a comeback of the Colorados and the Blancos, accompanied by a left-wing alliance, the Broad Front.

Designed to be weak

Under Uruguay's extraordinary constitution, different factions of the main parties can put up their own candidates in the election itself, rather than in a primary election. This virtually guarantees weak government. The winner of a presidential election in November 1984 was Jose Maria Sanguinetti, a highly articulate Colorado, with only 38.6% of the vote. Mr Sanguinetti tried to introduce free-market reforms and a balanced budget (mostly through spending cuts) by consensus. State employees went on strike to defend their jobs. In 1989 the free-market reformer Luis Alberto Lacalle, leader of a Blanco faction, won the presidential election with 37% of the vote. He too sought a national consensus for reforms, and failed. Factionalism predominated.

Society: dark memories

During Mr Sanguinetti's presidency there was a huge national debate over whether to grant an amnesty for soldiers and policemen accused of human-rights violations. The idea was to sweep the affair under the carpet on the understanding that, if untouched, the armed forces would stay out of politics. The debate ended in a referendum in 1989 which came out in favour of an amnesty.

Economy: slow improvement

The economy is based on services. Among these are: banking; tourism, especially in Punta del Este; some modest industries; and cattle and grains in the interior. Apart from its shortage of natural resources, Uruguay's problem is its swollen state sector (some 270,000 employees in a workforce of 1.2m of whom 80,000 are said to be surplus to requirements). Taxpayers have to pay for some 600,000 pensions. Some articulate, well-educated and unionised state employees are well aware that the economic reforms that the country needs will throw many of them out of work. The reforms, including privatisation, have been partly blocked. Mr Lacalle suffered a major defeat when his plans to enable the privatisation of ANTEL, the state communications company, were rejected in a referendum. Nonetheless, inflation was brought down from 112% in 1990 to 54.1% in 1993, the budget was more or less balanced in 1993, and GDP grew by 2% (although this was a sharp fall from growth of 7% in 1992). There is a large trade deficit, but this is covered by earnings from tourism, as well as lower payments to service the foreign debt because of low interest rates.

Total area	176,220 sq km	% agricultural area	86
Capital	Montevideo	Highest point metres	Cerro
Other cities	Sato, Paysandu,		Mirador 501
	Las Piedras	Main rivers	Uruguay, Negro

The economy

GDP $bn	10.4	GDP per head $	3,340
% av. ann. growth in		GDP per head in purchasing	
real GDP 1987–92	2.5	power parity (USA=100)	30.1

Origins of GDP	*% of total*	**Components of GDP**	*% of total*
Agriculture	10	Private consumption	70
Industry	32	Public consumption	13
of which:		Investment	13
manufacturing	25	Exports	24
Services	58	Imports	-21

Structure of manufacturing

% of total

Agric. & food processing	32	Other	41
Textiles & clothing	18	Av. ann. increase in industrial	
Machinery & transport	9	output 1987–92	...

Inflation and exchange rates

Consumer price 1993 av. ann. incr.	54.1%	Pesos per $ av. 1993	3.95
Av. ann. rate 1988–93	82.2%	Pesos per ecu av. 1993	4.42

Balance of payments, reserves, aid and debt

$bn

Visible exports fob	1.7	Capital balance	0.1
Visible imports fob	-1.9	Overall balance	-0.05
Trade balance	-0.2	Change in reserves	0.1
Invisible inflows	0.9	Level of reserves end Dec.	0.8
Invisible outflows	-0.9	Foreign debt	5.3
Net transfers	0.03	as % of GDP	46.8
Current account balance	-0.2	Debt service	
as % of GDP	-1.8	as % of export earnings	22.2

Principal exports	*$m fob*	**Principal imports**	*$m cif*
Textiles	461	Machinery & transport equip.	742
Hides	207	Chemicals	401
Beef	163	Oils & oil products	158
Cereals	181	Agricultural products	103

Main export destinations	*% of total*	**Main origins of imports**	*% of total*
Brazil	17.5	Brazil	23.7
Argentina	15.4	Argentina	17.3
USA	10.7	USA	9.4
EU	25.8	South Korea	6.1

Government

System Republic with directly elected president. Bicameral General Assembly consists of 31-member Senate and 99-member Chamber of Representatives.

Main political parties National Party, Colorado Party, Broad Front Coalition

Climate and topography

Warm and temperate. Mostly rolling plains and low hills. Fertile coastal lowland.

People and society

Population m	3.1	% under 15	25.8
Pop. per sq km	18	% over 65	11.4
% urban	86	No. men per 100 women	95
% av. ann. growth 1987–92	0.6	Human Development Index	88.1
No. households m	...		

Life expectancy	*yrs*	**Education**	
Men	69	Spending as % of GDP	3.3
Women	76	Years of compulsory education	8
Crude birth rate	17	Adult literacy %	96
Crude death rate	10	Primary school enrolment %	88
Infant mortality		Secondary school enrolment %	77
per 1,000 live births	23	Tertiary education enrolment %	...

Workforce	*% of total*	**Consumer goods ownership**	
			Pop. per
Services	67		
Industry	18	Car	13.9
Agriculture	15	TV	4.3
% unemployed	9.3	Telephone	6.1

Ethnic groups	*% of total*	**Religious groups**	*% of total*
White	88	Roman Catholic	66
Mestizo	8	Protestant	2
Black	4	Jewish	2
		Other or non-professing	30

Tourism		**Health**	
Tourist arrivals m	1.3	Pop. per doctor	510
Tourist receipts $bn	0.3		

VENEZUELA

Total area	912,050 sq km	Population	20.3m
GDP	$58.9bn	GDP per head	$2,900
Capital	Caracas	Other cities	Maracaibo, Valencia

With its vast oil riches and its proximity to the United States, Venezuela has become an important country for trading and investment. The country is a model for others in respecting its democratic rules. But after two decades of poor government, economic upheavals and rising expectations, the political atmosphere is volatile.

History: a poor beginning

Before the Spaniards arrived, large areas of Venezuela were inhabited by indigenous peoples living in the Andes, the Orinoco delta and the Guayana jungles. Christopher Columbus discovered it in 1498. A year later Alonso de Ojeda found Lake Maracaibo and, fascinated by the houses which the local inhabitants built on stilts in it, called the area "little Venice", or Venezuela. African slaves provided much-needed labour for the sugar plantations that were developed along the Caribbean coast. The Spanish settlers regarded themselves as an elite, but few had noble ancestry or could claim to be gentlemen; many were farmers, poor traders and smugglers.

Bolivar's moment

After defeating the Spanish army in a long war (1810–21), Simon Bolivar, the liberator, created Greater Colombia out of Venezuela, Colombia, Ecuador, Bolivia and Peru. He dominated Venezuelan affairs until 1830. Bolivar was succeeded by an illiterate but cunning rebel general, Jose Antonio Paez. There was subsequently a struggle for power in which some 350,000 men are said to have been killed. Venezuela enjoyed stable government under three strongmen: Antonio Guzman (1870–88), Juan Vicente Gomez (1908–35) and Marcos Perez Jimenez (1948–58). From 1945 to 1948 the country was ruled by a civilian democrat, Romulo Betancourt, at the head of a junta. This was ousted by Perez Jimenez. Betancourt subsequently won a free election as the candidate of his party, Democratic Action (AD), and ruled again from 1959 to 1964. To many Latin Americans he personified the merits of social democracy in contrast not only to the communism of Fidel Castro but also to the military dictatorships in many countries of the region. Supporters of Betancourt, an inveterate pipe-smoker, used to chant: "Pipe Yes! Beard No!"

Thereafter Venezuela had an impressive democratic record: Raul Leoni (1964–69); the populist Rafael Caldera of the opposition Social Christians (COPEI) (1969–74); the AD's Carlos Andres Perez (1974–79); COPEI's Luis Herrera Campins (1979–84); the AD's controversial Jaime Lusinchi (1984–89); Mr Perez again (1989–1993) and Mr Caldera again, after an interregnum, in 1994. But power had more or less alternated between two parties and it began to corrupt. A "political class" evolved in Caracas. As president followed president and huge profits from Venezuela's oil sales poured in, with nobody in Caracas making any effort, life seemed easy. Governments thought they could buy off special interests. Thus the poor were given food subsidies and cheap public transport. Manufacturers were given tariff protection. Banks were given a special exchange-rate deal.

Jobs for the boys

Political friends and enemies were given jobs in state enterprises (by 1980 there were 91 "administrative entities", 79 state-owned enterprises and 146 mixed private-and-public enterprises). One vast state enterprise, the Venezuelan Corporation of Guayana (CGV), built and controlled dams, electricity networks and aluminium plants. Its boss, Leopoldo Sucre Figarella, was almost a power unto himself. President Perez had, in 1976, nationalised the oil industry through the state holding company Petroleos de Venezuela (PDVSA). Thereafter the government milked PDVSA for all it was worth. Judges were appointed on the basis of their politics rather than their competence. The water supply in Caracas was badly maintained. Much of the sewage of Caracas poured untreated down a river to the Caribbean. The police were underpaid, under-staffed and corrupt. Hospitals, on the other hand, were over-staffed as a result of feather-bedding in union contracts but, since there was never enough money, the staff were underpaid and incompetent.

Debt crisis

Regardless of the country's oil income, Venezuela and PDVSA had to borrow from the banks to pay their bills. Under President Herrera Campins the bills began coming in from the banks as the world oil price slipped. Venezuela, incredibly, could not pay. In 1983 the government declared a partial moratorium on public-sector debt servicing and refused to release the foreign exchange for servicing the private-sector debt. Prolonged negotiation in 1986–87 ended with an agreement to delay payments to the banks.

Perez is converted

In his second term, President Perez made a U-turn from his old spendthrift ways. He launched a tough restructuring programme. While out of office he had become convinced that the IMF's approach would be right for Venezuela. He cut import tariffs from an average of 37% in 1988 to 12.5% in 1992 in order to open up the economy and make it competitive. He devalued the currency, making it competitive. Non-traditional exports surged. He cut subsidies and government spending in general, slashing the fiscal deficit. Venezuela signed a debt-restructuring agreement with the commercial banks in 1990 covering $19.8 billion.

The reforms hurt badly at first: GDP fell by 8.6% in 1989. But the economy bounced back as confidence returned, growing by 6.3% in 1990, a remarkable 9.7% in 1991 and 6.8% in 1992. The government's weakness was that it did not have enough tax revenues to cover spending because Congress blocked a proposed value-added tax. It also blocked a general law authorising the president to privatise state enterprises.

Too much of a statesman

But Mr Perez paid too much attention to his role as a regional statesman and too little to the need to provide Venezuelans with good government. Venezuelans wanted more law and order, and public services which worked. Calls grew for his resignation before the end of his constitutional term, especially from ex-President Rafael Caldera, who had ambitions of his own. Another old political rival moved to impeach the president on a charge of misappropriating public funds. A $17m secret presidential fund was handled carelessly although there was no clear evidence that Mr Perez had profited personally (some of the money apparently went to help President Violeta Chamorro of Nicaragua to oppose the leftist Sandinists). By the end of 1992 there had been two unsuccessful attempts at a military coup against Mr Perez. Congress, which had blocked many of his reforms, suspended him in May 1992 and replaced him in June by Senator Ramon Jose Velasquez.

Caldera comes back

Mr Velasquez made substantial changes during his short period in office. He won congressional approval for the imposition of VAT and a framework bill to extend privatisation. He also replaced Mr Sucre Figarella of the CVG. The presidential election in December 1993 was peaceful and well-ordered. It was won by Mr Caldera, then 77, with 30%

Government

System Republic. President is elected directly for a term of 5 years. Bicameral Congress of the Republic consists of Senate and Chamber of Deputies.
Main political parties Organising Committee of the Independent Electoral Party (COPEI), Democratic Action, Movement Toward Socialism

Climate and topography

Tropical; hot and humid but more moderate in highlands. Andes mountains and Maracaibo lowlands in northwest, central plains, highlands in southeast.

People and society

Population m	20.3	% under 15	34.7
Pop. per sq km	24	% over 65	4.1
% urban	91	No. men per 100 women	102
% av. ann. growth 1987–92	2.4	Human Development Index	82.4
No. households m	3.8		

Life expectancy	*yrs*	**Education**	
Men	67	Spending as % of GDP	4.1
Women	74	Years of compulsory education	...
Crude birth rate	27	Adult literacy %	88
Crude death rate	4	Primary school enrolment %	61
Infant mortality		Secondary school enrolment %	35
per 1,000 live births	23	Tertiary education enrolment %	28

Workforce	*% of total*	**Consumer goods ownership**	
Services	56		*Pop. per*
Industry	32	Car	10.6
Agriculture	12	TV	6.0
% unemployed	7.1	Telephone	10.9

Ethnic groups	*% of total*	**Religious groups**	*% of total*
Mestizo	67	Roman Catholic	96
White	21	Protestant	2
Black	10		
Indian	2		

Tourism		**Health**	
Tourist arrivals m	0.5	Pop. per doctor	700
Tourist receipts $bn	0.4		

Glossary

AD Accion Democratica. Venezuela's formerly dominant political party, Democratic Action. Founded by Romulo Betancourt. Fared badly in 1993 elections.
ALADI Latin American Integration Association. Founded in Montevideo (Uruguay) in 1980 to replace the Latin American Free Trade Assciation. Encourages region-wide free-trade. Superseded to a certain extent by sub-regional free-trade groupings.
Altiplano High-altitude land mostly in Bolivia where farmers scratch a living. Has produced its own genre of folk music played on local instruments.
Andean Group Founded in 1969 by the Andean Pact. Based in Lima, it comprises Bolivia, Colombia, Ecuador, Venezuela and Peru. Chile withdrew in 1976. Committed to sub-regional integration. Originally somewhat hostile to foreign investors. Led to separate free-trade areas linking Venezuela and Colombia and, later, Ecuador.
Andes Mountain range (*Cordillera de los Andes*) stretching from southern Chile to Colombia.
APRA Alianza Popular Revolucionaria Americana. Peru's American Popular Revolutionary Alliance. Influential party kept in opposition by fair means and foul except for the disastrous presidency of Alan Garcia.
Atacama Hilly desert, like a moonscape, in north Chile.
Aymara Language used by many in Peru and Bolivia.
Bajan Inhabitant of Barbados.
Baker Plan Launched by President Reagan's secretary of the treasury, James Baker, to help heavily indebted Latin American governments. Those which carried out approved structural economic reforms were meant to receive an injection of commercial-bank money. The plan failed because the banks were unwilling to cough up "fresh money".
Basuco A cheap and often dangerous form of cocaine used by addicts in Colombia.
Brady Plan Launched by President Bush's secretary of the treasury, Nicholas Brady, to reduce the commercial-bank debt of Latin American countries using various techniques. Among them: selling debt paper at a discount, converting the debt paper to units of the same value but a lower interest rate, and reducing the face value but maintaining the interest rate. Had considerable success.
Cairns Group Some 14 unsubsidised agricultural exporters including Argentina and Brazil and led by Australia. Lobbies hard against America's farm subsidies and the EU's Common Agricultural Policy.
Caribbean Development Bank Regional development

bank based in Bridgetown (Barbados). Its president is Sir Neville Nicholls. Has responsibility for analysing the economies of the islands in annual reports, making policy recommendations and granting development loans.

CARICOM The Caribbean Community and Common Market. Based in Georgetown (Guyana), it comprises 18 members, two associate members and six observers. Founded in 1973 as a force for unity in the Caribbean. By 1994 all but one member of the Common Market had agreed to a common external tariff.

Carioca Inhabitant of Rio de Janeiro.

Carnaval Shrove Tuesday, before the start of Lent, when merry-making Cariocas and people in several other regional cities may lose their remaining inhibitions. Rio's *carnaval* is marked by an intense competition among the city's "samba schools".

Central American Common Market Founded in 1960 with a headquarters in Guatemala City by the Organisation of Central American States, it comprised El Salvador, Guatemala, Honduras, Nicaragua and Costa Rica. Based on import substitution and planned industrial development. Lapsed after war between El Salvador and Honduras. Integration was revived in the early 1990s by free-trade pacts between Guatemala and El Salvador, later joined by Honduras and Nicaragua. By 1994 the new pact was begining to work.

Chaco, or **Gran Chaco** Mostly barren flatlands stretching from south-eastern Bolivia across western Paraguay to northern Argentina.

Christian Democrats Politicians usually of the centre-left to centre-right with links to the Roman Catholic church who have, from time to time, through their own parties ruled Chile, Venezuela, Costa Rica and El Salvador.

COPEI The curiously named Comite Organizador del Partido Electoral Independiente (Organising Committee of the Independent Electoral Party). Venezuelan political party linked to the Christian Democratic movement. One of two leading parties since the return of democracy in 1959.

Cuba libre Free Cuba. Also, a rum and coke.

Distrito Federal Federal Districts cover the capitals of Brazil (Brasilia) and Mexico (Mexico city).

ECLAC The UN's Economic Commission for Latin America and the Caribbean. Based in Santiago and respected for its annual Economic Survey on the state of the region's economy and its preliminary overview as well as for its analyses of socio-economic trends. Makes policy recommendations.

Gringo Citizen of the United States. Also, in the eyes of prejudiced Latin Americans, a vulgar, loud-mouthed, aggressive, materialistic and otherwise uncultured person.
Guarani Language used predominantly in Paraguay along with Spanish.
IDB Inter-American Development Bank. Based in Washington, it comprises 44 regional and non-regional members. President is Enrique Iglesias, a respected former executive secretary of ECLAC and Uruguayan foreign minister. Apart from the IMF and World Bank, it is the major lender to regional governments. Has expanded its role to include loans linked to economic policies as well as to specific projects.
IMF International Monetary Fund. Founded in 1945 in Washington to serve as the world's bank manager. Now plays a key role in international lending to Latin America and the Caribbean – but only on terms negotiated between the Fund and the borrower.
Justicialista Correct name of Argentina's Peronist party. The party's philosophy is known as Justicialismo
Latifundia Big estate, usually employing numerous poor and landless farm-workers.
Llanos Plains. More specifically, the plains stretching from north-eastern Colombia across central Venezuela.
Macho Overly assertive male. Species found in many parts of Latin America.
Manana Tomorrow. When the delivery will be made, the contract will be signed, the car will be repaired, the plumber will come and other promises will be kept.
Mato Grosso Plateau in west-central Brazil long neglected because of poor communications and now being developed. Temperatures often hot. Grasslands, woods and scrub, good for livestock and some farming. Deposits of iron ore, manganese and tin.
Minifundia Smallholding, frequently not large enough to support a family adequately. In Bolivia, created by the break-up of *latifundias* in 1952.
MNR Movimiento Nacional Revolucionario. Bolivia's National Revolutionary Movement. Presided over a social revolution in 1952 and a drastic – and successful – economic reform in 1985.
Organisation of American States (OAS) Established at Washington in 1948 to promote hemispheric co-operation. Comprises all countries of the region except Cuba, which was suspended in 1962. Often dismissed as an American-dominated talking shop. It can ask members to impose sanctions on regional governments or send in a peace-

making force to restore order in a civil war – and has done so.
Organisation of Eastern Caribbean States Set up to promote co-operation between islands of the sub-region. Sent a small force to accompany American units to restore order in Grenada in 1983.
Pampas Argentina's prairies.
PAN Partido de Accion Nacional. Mexico's small but growing conservative National Action Party.
Paris Club Name given to *ad hoc* set-up under which official government creditors negotiate with indebted countries, including many from Latin America, over debt-servicing arrangements and the extension of official credits.
Patagonia Mostly semi-arid, chilly and windy plateau in south Argentina, with farming in the less punishing north.
Paulista Inhabitant of Sao Paulo.
Porteno Inhabitant of Buenos Aires.
PMDB Partido Movimento Democratico Brasileiro. Founded during the military dictatorship as an opposition group, the right-of-centre Brazilian Democratic Movement Party was in 1994 the biggest party in parliament.
PRI Mexico's Institutional Revolutionary Party. Has ruled the country since the 1920s and has frequently been accused of corruption, electoral fraud and of being identified with and financed by the government.
PT Partido dos Trabalhadores. Brazil's union-backed, leftish Workers' Party led by Luiz Inacio ("Lula") da Silva. Calls for greater social justice for Brazil's poor masses.
Quechua Language widely used in Bolivia and Peru.
Rio Group Twelve Latin American presidents who form the group meet regularly to discuss regional issues and attitudes toward the United States and Europe.
Rio Treaty Signed in 1947 by the United States and Latin American governments, excluding Cuba, the treaty, officially known as the Inter-American Treaty on Reciprocal Assistance, was a cold-war pact intended to protect signatories from communist attacks.
Saudade Untranslateable Brazilian-Portuguese word combining nostalgia, sadness and yearning for a past pleasure or love.
Serra Geral de Goias Prairies of central Brazil where wheat and soya is increasingly grown.
World Bank Officially the International Bank for Reconstruction and Development. Founded in 1945 in Washington to help the reconstruction of post-wear Europe it has transferred its lending activities for economic development to the third world and plays a central role in lending to Latin America and the Caribbean.

Notes on data

For a list of the main sources used in preparing this book see page 200.

Coverage

The extent and quality of the statistics available vary from country to country. Every care has been taken to specify the broad definitions on which the data are based and to indicate cases where data quality or technical difficulties are such that interpretation of the figures is likely to be seriously affected. Nevertheless, figures from individual countries will often differ from standard international statistical definitions.

Statistical basis

The research for this section was carried out in 1994 using the latest published sources. The data, therefore, unless otherwise indicated, refer to the year ending December 31st 1992. Exceptions are: population under 15 and over 65, number of men per 100 women and urban population which refer to estimates for 1991; crude birth and death rates and life expectancy are based on 1985–90 averages; GDP per head in PPP and tourism refer to 1991; structure of manufacturing and household, consumer goods and expenditure data refer to 1991; ethnic groups, marriage and divorce, education and health data refer to the latest year with available figures.

Figures may not add exactly to totals, or percentages to 100, because of rounding. Sums of money have generally been converted to US dollars at the official exchange rate ruling at the time to which the figures refer.

Definitions

Agricultural area The area of arable land, land under permanent crops and pasture land expressed as a percentage of a country's total area.

Balance of payments The record of a country's transactions with the rest of the world. The **current account** of the balance of payments consists of: exports of visible trade (goods) less imports of visible trade; "invisible" trade: receipts and payments for services such as banking, tourism and shipping plus dividend and interest payments and profit remittances; private transfer payments, such as remittances from those working abroad; official transfers, including payments to international organisations and some current expenditure aid flows (such as famine relief). Visible imports and exports are normally compiled on rather different definitions to those used in the trade statistics (shown in principal imports and exports) and therefore the statistics do not match. The **capital account** consists of long- and short-term transactions relating to a country's assets and liabilities (for example loans and borrowings). Adding the current to the capital account gives the overall balance. This is compensated by net monetary movements and changes in reserves. In practice methods of statistical recording are neither complete nor accurate and an errors and omissions item, sometimes quite large, will appear. In the country facts pages of this book this item is included in the overall balance. Changes in reserves are shown without the practice of reversing the sign often followed in balance of payments presentations. They exclude monetary movements and therefore do not equal the overall balance.

Cif/fob When goods pass through customs and are recorded in trade statistics they are normally registered at their value at the point of passage through customs. Imports, which are valued at the point of entry to a country, will include the cost of "carriage, insurance and freight" (cif) from the exporting country to the importing one. The value of exports does not include these elements and is recorded "free on board" (fob). The value of imports will therefore automatically be greater than the equivalent amount of exports – in many cases by a factor of 10–12%. In most (but not all) countries the crude trade statistics record imports cif and exports fob; balance of payments statistics are generally adjusted so that imports are shown fob.

Crude birth rate The number of live births in a year per 1,000 population. The crude rate will automatically be relatively high if a large proportion of the population is of childbearing age and low if this is not the case.

Crude death rate The number of deaths in one year per 1,000 population. Like the crude birth rate this is affected by the population's age structure. It will be relatively high if there is a high proportion of old people in the population.

Debt, foreign Financial obligations owed by a country to the rest of the world and repayable in foreign currency. **Debt service** consists of interest payments on outstanding debt plus any principal repayments due. **The debt service ratio** is debt service expressed as a percentage of the country's earnings from exports of goods and services.

Enrolment ratio (gross) The number enrolled at a specific level of education, whether or not they belong to the age group relevant to that level, as a percentage of the total population in the relevant age group. The ratio can therefore be over 100% if children start an education stage early or stay in it late; conversely, a ratio below 100% can be consistent with full education if children of the appropriate age group have passed on early to the following stage.

GDP Gross Domestic Product. It is the sum of all output produced by economic activity within that country. Economic activity normally refers to goods and services that are exchanged for money or traded in a market system (activities such as housework, childcare by parents and household repairs or improvements carried out by occupiers are excluded). Subsistence farming and other activities that could potentially be exchanged for money are theoretically also included but national statistics vary in the extent to which they cover them.

GDP can be measured in three ways: by summing the output of all production (origins of GDP); by measuring all expenditure on a country's production and adding stockbuilding (components of GDP); or by measuring the income of businesses and individuals generated by the production of goods and services. The exports and imports figures shown in national accounts statistics are defined differently from visible and invisible exports and imports used in the balance of payments, notably by excluding interest, profits and dividends payments.

GDP can be measured either at "market prices", the prices at which goods and services are bought by consumers, or at "factor cost", the cost of producing an item excluding taxes and subsidies. In general the expenditure breakdown is shown at market prices and the production breakdown at factor cost. Data on total GDP generally refer to market prices. National income is obtained by deducting an estimate of depreciation of capital goods (capital consumption) from GDP.

The average annual increase in real GDP shows the growth in GDP excluding any increase due solely to the rise in prices.

Human Development Index This new index is an attempt by the United Nations Development Programme to assess relative levels of human development in various countries. It combines three measures: life expectancy, literacy and whether the average income, based on purchasing power parity (PPP) estimates (see below), is sufficient to meet basic needs. For each component a country's score is scaled according to where it falls between the minimum and maximum country scores; for income adequacy the maximum is taken as the official "poverty line" incomes in nine industrial countries. The scaled scores on the three measures are averaged to give the Human Development Index, shown here scaled from 0 to 100. Countries scoring less than 50 are classified as low human development, those from 50 to 80 as medium and those above 80 as high.

As with any statistical exercise of this sort the results are subject to caveats and the small number of indicators used places some limitations on its usefulness. The index should not be taken as a quality of life indicator since in particular it excludes any direct notion of freedom.

Inflation The rate at which prices are increasing. The most common measure and the one shown here (but not the only one) is to take the increase in the consumer price index.

Life expectancy rates refer to the average length of time a baby born today can expect to live.

PPP Purchasing Power Parity. Comparing GDP per head is an unsatisfactory way of comparing relative living standards since it does not take account of differences in prices of goods and services (the cost of living). PPP statistics adjust for cost of living differences by replacing normal exchange rates with rates designed to equalize the prices of a standard "basket" of goods and services. These are used to obtain PPP estimates of GDP per head. PPP estimates are normally shown on a scale of 1–100, taking the USA, where the average standard of living is highest, as 100. World Bank PPP estimates have been used in this book.

Real terms Figures adjusted to allow for inflation.

Unemployment ratio The number of unemployed people expressed as a percentage of a country's total workforce.

Abbreviations

Aladi Latin American Integration Association
bn billion (one thousand million)
GDP Gross Domestic Product
GNP Gross National Product
kg kilogram
km kilometre
m million
PPP Purchasing Power Parity
– zero
... not available

Sources

EIU, *Country Reports*
Encyclopedia Britannica
The Europa World Yearbook
IMF, *Balance of Payments Yearbook*
IMF, *International Financial Statistics*
International Labor Office, *Yearbook of Labor Statistics*
Statesmen's Year-Book
United Nations, *World Population Prospects*
US Central Intelligence Agency, *World Factbook*
World Bank, *World Debt Tables*
World Bank, *World Development Report*

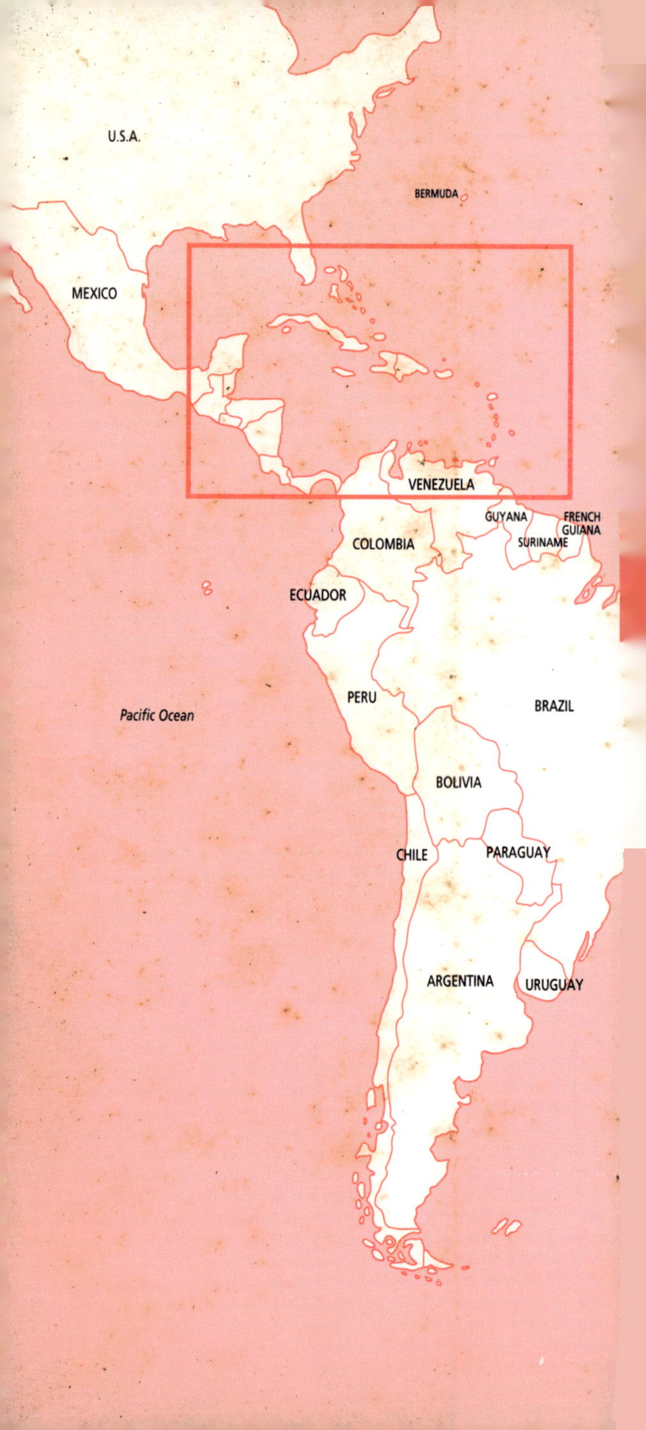
U.S.A.
BERMUDA
MEXICO
VENEZUELA
GUYANA
FRENCH GUIANA
SURINAME
COLOMBIA
ECUADOR
PERU
BRAZIL
Pacific Ocean
BOLIVIA
CHILE
PARAGUAY
ARGENTINA
URUGUAY